Step by Step Beginners Guide to Learn Programming

The Complete Introduction Guide for Learning the Basics of C, C#, C++, SQL, JAVA, JAVASCRIPT, PHP, and PYTHON.

A Pratical Programming Language Course

By

Kevin Cooper

Table of Contents

9

versions of the work, physical, digital, and audio unless express consent of the Publisher is provided beforehand. Any additional rights reserved.

Furthermore, the information that can be found within the pages described forthwith shall be considered both accurate and truthful when it comes to the recounting of facts. As such, any use, correct or incorrect, of the provided information will render the Publisher free of responsibility as to the actions taken outside of their direct purview. Regardless, there are zero scenarios where the original author or the Publisher can be deemed liable in any fashion for any damages or hardships that may result from any of the information discussed herein.

Additionally, the information in the following pages is intended only for informational purposes and should thus be thought of as universal. As befitting its nature, it is presented without assurance regarding its prolonged validity or interim quality. Trademarks that are mentioned are done without written consent and can in no way be considered an endorsement from the trademark holder.

Chapter One: Introduction to Programming

Thank you for buying this book because it is the best investment you will make in improving your skill as a programmer. The book contains information on the basics of programming in various programming languages including PHP, JavaScript, Java, Python, SQL, C+, C#, and C.

I am Kevin Cooper and if you are a beginner, do not worry because I started the same way as you are about to do. I will be your driver and guide for this wonderful journey of the beginners' guide to learning programming.

The book is geared towards you understanding the aforementioned programming languages in its simplicity. I will teach you in a way that you will not forget. The book contains exercises, which is important for you to practice if you want to be a productive and successful programmer.

Today, we have seen hundreds of programming languages created for different purposes. However, we have also seen some of these programming languages gaining more popularity over others.

No matter what your quest is, welcome to the world of programming where everything is possible. Programming is simply the act or process of writing programs to instruct the computer what actions to perform or not. These programs use various series of instructions in a particular language (all language have different instruction). Nevertheless, in this book, you learn the fundamentals of seven programming languages. These languages include C, C++, C#, SQL, Java, PHP, and Python.

Programming isn't complicated as many try to portray it. If that has been your perception, this step by step beginners' guide to learn programming will change that perception. It is surely going to be a fun ride as long as you stick to what is contained in this book. I am confident this book contains everything you need as a beginner, who is looking forward to going into advanced coding. Let's crack the nuts together.

What is a Programming Language?

In layman's term, this is an artificial language aimed at controlling the operation and functionality of a computer. It is akin to our English language, which we use to express our ideas. Just like there are rules in the English language, so it is with programming languages. They have rules (syntactic and semantic rules), which programmers must adhere to

To understand it better, an example will clarify everything. Assuming you met someone on the way and he/she asked for the nearest bank. What would be your response to the person? How will you describe the direction in such a way that the person never forgets? Obviously, you will do something like this:

- Take the straight path towards you for 1 kilometer
- Take the right turn at the traffic light
- Then drive for another half kilometer
- At your right-hand side is the bank

This is an instruction in the English language and it followed a particular sequence for the person to follow in order to get to the bank. For a moment, what will be the situation if the same case scenario is a computer program? As simple as the direction is, you can write programs for this example using any programming language of your choice. However, you won't use your daily English language words but those understood by the computer.

A program, also called software sometimes contains a couple of lines to millions of lines with each providing different instructions. The instructions are called source code whereas the act of writing codes is known as program coding. It doesn't matter how the body of a system looks, without a program, the computer can do nothing. The program gives life to the computer when you power it on.

Just as we have different languages in the world, computer scientists have developed various languages but with the primary purpose of writing computer programs. There are over a hundred programming languages available for anyone to learn. It is hard to learn everything but it is important to have basic knowledge of the important once.

Building a Foundation for Writing Codes

Programming languages are geared towards solving a particular problem. Yes, you want to be a problem solver by creating important product and services but irrespective of how you practice, there are essential skills you must possess. Learning programming will offer you numerous job opportunities and increase your wages while working for fewer hours. Coders or developers spend time making applications, websites, and systems work together in order to improve the experience of their employers and end-users. Welcome to the Programming industry where there is no impossibility as long as you can envision it. However, there are important skills you must have before starting this journey.

- **Self-Reliance** – This skill is huge because as a beginner, you may feel overwhelmed. You will be confronted with various decisions to make such as what language to learn? Should I focus on the back end or front end? Where do I start? At times, you will feel like giving up after hours of no sleep without any significant progress. However, you do not have to give up. Success doesn't come cheap, there is a price to pay. To be a successful programmer, you have to master distraction, frustrations, impatience, and be self-reliance to accept the responsibility at hand.

- **Attention to details** – If you want to excel as a beginner, you must have attention to the minimum detail. Everything matters in programming. A single spelling can cause your program to go wrong if you are not painstaking in paying attention to details. You don't have to work round the clock; take some time off and refresh yourself in you want to up and doing. Make your own research, make your own notes, and continue to improve yourself.

- **Abstract thinking** – Programmers are thinkers, who think outside the box. They are not confined to a particular solution. They have their perspective on a global level, seeing things from a different angle in order to find ways of improving on what already exists.

- **Patience** – Whoever tells you coding is easy is lying because you have to dedicate time, resource to come up with solutions. At some stage, you should expect some level of frustration because things may not go the way you wanted. At times, you may feel useless and the project isn't worth the time, however in such a situation, you have to be patient. Every successful programmer has undergone through these challenges. Patience is the key to writing codes. According to Steve Jobs, " It's worth waiting to get it right" Therefore, no matter the challenge, let patience be the key.

Chapter Two: Learning C Programming Language

Introduction

The C programming language is one of the most commonly used languages with various versions developed over the years. The C language is the fundamental language to understand before considering learning the C# and C++ language. My goal in this chapter is to enable you to have the fundamental knowledge concerning the basics of C programming language including the various data types.

Before starting, it is important to familiarize yourself with the language. The C programming language is also referred to as a general-purpose because programmers can use it for varieties of application. Its popularity is linked to its efficiency despite how old it has been in existence. Most C programs are portable, which means that a code written in a particular system can work in another operating system.

Features of C Programming Language

It is significant to identify certain features of the C language.

- **Fast** – New programming languages including Java and Python provides more features than C language.

Nevertheless, in terms of performance, they are lower to C.

- **Modularity** – This feature is unique as you can store C code in the form of libraries for future purposes. The language comes with its own standard libraries that you can use to solve various problems. Assuming you want something to display on the screen, you can use the "studio.h" library, which enables you to use the print f() function.

- **Portable** – Have you heard the statement, "Write once, compile everywhere." Yes, it is true with C programs because a program written in one system with Mac OS can be compiled in another system for instance Windows 7 without any change to the program.

Other features include reliability, interactivity, efficiency, and effectiveness.

Why Learn C Programming Language?

Perhaps, you are thinking, of what use is the C programming language today? Is it the only accessible programming language to users? Definitely, there are other languages you can learn, which are way higher and modern when compared to the C language.

However, there are important reasons most people choose to learn this programming language. Firstly, the C programming language preexisted before most of the computer languages you have thought about. There are unlimited resources to tap from the program with numerous functions to meet every programming need.

Secondly, most people still learn the language because it is hard for anyone not to get the solution they desire. It doesn't have to take you years to learn a particular programming language. The internet has even made it easier as there are thousands of free tutorials to learn the language.

Thirdly, the C programming language is the language used by UNIX. Interestingly, UNIX is one of the leading computer software in the world. Besides, other operating systems also take advantage of the simplicity of the programming language. Importantly, the way the language expresses ideas to make it easier for anyone to implement the language without requiring any aid.

If you are not still convinced, then it is imperative for me to indicate that the C programming language is the foundation for other programming languages, which is why we started this book with the language. For instance, there are certain commands and principles you will see here that are applicable to other programming languages.

For a newbie, C programming is the best to start your programming learning process. However, for an easier language to understand, you can go for Python, which I will talk about towards the end of this book.

Uses of Programming Language

Interestingly, you can use the C language for creating various system applications, which is an integral aspect of several operating systems including Linux, Windows, and UNIX. The following are areas where C is used.

- Interpreters
- Network drivers
- Spreadsheets
- Graphic packages
- Operating system development
- Database systems
- Compiler and assemblers

Setting Up the Environment

In learning a new language, you have to set up the environment to run the programs. In learning the C programming language, one should start from the basics before going to the complex aspects.

If you want to take this quest seriously, then you should begin by downloading and installing the C compiler. In computer programming, compilers are simply programs that read code and generate executable programs that a computer can understand.

The compiler is necessary as it reads the code you input and converts it to a computer-friendly signal.

There is no universal compiler because some programs can work in a certain operating system while the same cannot be said for others. However, the following suggestions will help you. If you are using a Window computer, you can install MinGW or Microsoft Visual Studio Express. However, for Mac and Linux operating system, you can use XCode and GCC respectively.

Besides a compiler, you will need a text editor to start coding. The compiler and text editor has different roles.

The role of the text editor is for you to type your program. There are various text editors available such as notepad, Emacs, OS Edit, etc. if you use a text editor, you create a source file, which has the source code. C programs have their file extension as ".c"

Once you complete your program in the text editor, the next thing is to save it. After undergoing the compilation process, you can execute it. The role of the compiler is to make the file you created usably. The compiler will make the source code created in the text editor readable for human.

Pre-requisite for Learning C

Unlike some programming languages that require you to study another language, C language is different. There is no prerequisite for learning the C programming the language. You don't require a preknowledge of data structures, algorithms, or even Boolean logic. However, with the basic knowledge of computers and logical skills, it is enough to begin your journey of learning C. Get the compiler installed on your computer and stay dedicated and surely you will be good at it over time.

As a professional programmer, I will advise you before beginning with this book, you should endeavor to understand basic computer programming terminologies as it will fast track your learning process.

Understanding the Basics

It is essential to identify the structure of a C program because without that your foundation in this language will be shaky. Getting yourself set up with these basics will help you a lot, as it will be a reference point to certain things I will explain in this book. The following are the basic structures:

- **Documentation section** – This section provides comments concerning the program, the author's name, the date it was created, the modification date, etc.
- **Link Section** – This includes header files necessary to execute program
- **Definition Section** – In this section, variable declaration and assignment of values are done.
- **Global Declaration Section** – Global variables are usually highlighted here. When you want to use a variable

throughout the program, you define them at the global declaration section.

- **Function prototype declaration section** – This section gives details about the various function such as parameter names, return types used within the function

- **Main function** – All C programs must originate from the main function. Primarily, it comprises of two different sections – the execution and the declaration sections.

- **User-defined function** – These sections contain functions defined by the users to perform a certain task.

Don't worry because it may look "foreign" to you as a beginner. However, I like to use examples to highlight my points. Assuming you want to write "Hello, Welcome to C Programming Language for Beginners" what code will you use to produce these words?

C Program Commands	Explanation
#include<stdio.h>	This preprocessor command contains the standard input-output header contained in the C library before the compilation of the program.
int main ()	This function indicates where the program execution begins
{	This specifies the starting

	point of a function
/* comments*/	Whatever is written between the /*...*/ is disregarded by the compiler because it serves as an explanation or comments.
Printf("Hello, Welcome to C Programming Language for Beginners");	The Printf command displays "Hello, Welcome to C Programming Language for Beginners" to the screen
Getch();	The command waits for the user to input any character of their choice from the console
Return 0;	This ends the main function of the program while returning 0
}	The closing brace specifies the ending point of the main function

Let's assume you want the following statement to show on the screen. "Hello, Welcome to C Programming Language for Beginners" on the screen, it will be as follow.

```
#include <stdio.h>
/* the int main () is the part where the execution of the program
```

```
begins*/
Int main ()
{
        /* Performing the First Programming Sample in C
language*/
        Printf("Hello, Welcome to C Programming Language for
Beginners");
        Getch();
        Return 0;
}
```

Output

**Hello, Welcome to C Programming Language for
Beginners**

To ensure you write a program in C language and get the output, there are important steps to follow. There is no exception to these steps as far as it is a C program. It doesn't matter if it is a small or large program. These involve the creation, compilation, execution (running), and outputting of the program. For you to do this there are certain prerequisites

- You must have a C compiler installed on your system. With this, you can execute programs.

- It is not compulsory to install one on your system as you can instead use an online compiler to compile and execute your programs. Just search for online compilers for C and you will get more details.

Data Types

A data type is a very simple but important concept to understand in any programming language. It is a representation of a particular type of data, which is processed through a computer program. A particular data type determines a storage space along with the manner the bit pattern is understood when processing the data.

In C language, data types are categorized into four different groups

Types	Data Types
Enumeration data type	Enum
Basic Data	Int, float, char, double
Derived data type	Pointer, array, union, structure
Void data type	Void

Basic Data Types

Integer Data Type

This data type enables a user to use a variable to store numerical values. It is represented by the keyword "int" with storage size ranging from 2, 4, or 8 bytes. However, the integer data type varies depending on the processor you are using. For instance, if the computer is a 16-bit processor system, the int data type will be allocated 2-byte memory.

Character Data Type

This type of data type allows the variable to store only a character. Unlike the int, the char data type has a storage size of 1. This means that you can only store a particular character for the data type. The character keyword is represented by the "char" keyword.

Float Data Type

These comprise of two types – the float and double data type

Float – this allows you to store decimal values with a storage size of 4. However, the storage size varies from one processor of a computer to another. On the other hand, the double is identical to the float data type. After the decimal value, the double data type allows as far as -10 digits.

Enumeration Data type

This data type comprises of named integer constants in the form of a list. By default, it begins with 0 with the value increasing by 1 for the consecutive identifies within its list. The syntax for Enum in C programming language is:

enum identifier [{enumerator-list}];

Derived Data Type

These data types include array, structure, pointer, and union.

Void data type

This type of data type does not have a value and used in pointers and functions.

Keywords, Identifiers (Variables), and Literals

In C language, we have a character set, which includes a set of alphabets, letters, and some special characters. The alphabets comprise of those in upper and lower case. Note that the alphabets "A and a" are not the same – C language is case sensitive.

Keywords are reserved words in programming that has its own distinct connotation to the compiler. They are an integral aspect of the syntax of the language that cannot be used as an identifier. For instance:

int number;

In this example, the word "int" is a reserved keyword, which indicates that number is a variable of integer type. The table below shows the keywords allowed in C language

volatile	void	unsigned	while
typedef	struct	union	switch
size	signed	short	static
register	int	return	long
goto	for	float	if
enum	double	extern	else
default	continue	const	do
case	auto	char	break

Identifiers are names given to entities like functions, variables, structures, etc. They are unique and created to an entity within the execution of the program. For instance,

> **int Money;**
>
> **double accountBal;**

In the example above, money and accountable are identifiers. Remember identifiers must not be the same as keywords. How then do you form an identifier?

- An identifier can have letters, digits, and underscore. Letters can be both lowercase and uppercase.
- The first letter for an identifier must be an underscore or letter.
- A keyword cannot be used as an identifier

- There is no particular length for an identifier

Literals

These are values whose value cannot be changed in the course of the program. The term is used in place of constant, so when you see constant they mean the same thing. Constants comprise of various data types including integer, character, floating, and string.

An integer constant on no situation must have an exponential or fractional part. We have three integer literals in C programming. These are:

- Decimal (example: 54, -98, 11)
- Octal (example: 042, 089, 044)
- Hexadecimal (example: 0x9f, 0x345, 0x7a)

Floating-point literals are numerical literal with an exponent or fractional part. For instance, -4.0, 0.0000345, -0.44E-9.

Characters are literally formed by enclosing them with a single quotation mark. For instance: 't', 'h', '8', etc;

Finally, a string literal comprises of a sequence or collection of characters encircled in double quotation marks. For instance, "love", "C Programming", "Professional"

Operators in C Programming Language

Operators are symbols, which tell the compiler what particular operation to carry on a particular variable. In C language, we have long-range operators, which are used to execute several operations on variables or operands. I will explain the basic operators you should know as a beginner learning programming.

Arithmetic Operators

In C programming language, these operators perform mathematical operators namely addition, subtraction, division, multiplication. These can be executed on various numerical values.

Operator	Meaning	Example
+	Addition	A + C = 50
*	Multiplication	A * C = 10
-	Subtraction	A – C = 20
/	Division	A/C= 5
%	Modulo division	C/A =0
++	Increment by 1	C++
--	Decrement by 1	C--

Example 1

```
#include <stdio.h>
main()
```

```
{
int day1 = 31;
int  = day2;
int day3 ;
final = day1 + day2;
printf("First Line - Value of day3 is %d\n", day3 );
day3 = day1 – day2;
printf("Second Line - Value of day3 is %d\n", day3 );
day3 = day1 * day2;
printf("Third Line  - Value of day3 is %d\n", day3 );
day3 =  day1 / day2;
printf("Fourth Line - Value of day3 is %d\n", day3);
day3 = day1 % day2;
printf("Fifth Line - Value of day3 is %d\n", day3 );
day3 = day1 ++;
printf("Sixth Line - Value of day3 is %d\n", day3 );
day3 = day2--;
printf("Seventh Line  - Value of day3 is %d\n", day3);
}
```

If you compile this program and it executed successfully, your output will be as follows: First Line - Value of day3 is 51

Second Line - Value of day3 is 11

Third Line - Value of day3 is 620

Fourth Line - Value of day3 is 1

Fifth Line - Value of day3 is 5

Sixth Line - Value of day3 is 32

Seventh Line - Value of day3 is 19

Relational Operators

The role of these operators is to verify the relationship or association that exists between two different operands. The table below shows the basic relational operators in the C language. Assuming the value for loss and profit are "25" and "35" respectively.

Operator	Meaning	Example
==	This operator evaluates whether the value is equivalent or not to the second value on the right. If it is true, the condition turns out to be true.	loss==profit is evaluated as not true
>	The operator verifies if the left operand greater than that on the right side	From the value, loss >profit is false true
<	The operator verifies if the left operand is less than that of the right side	loss < profit is true

!=	The operator verifies if the operand on the left side fulfill the condition by not being equivalent to the one on right side	loss !=profit returns true
>=	This verifies if the left operand is either greater or equivalent to the right operand	loss>=profit returns not true
<=	This verifies if the operand on the left is either less or equivalent to the right operand	loss<=profit is true

The example below will make it clearer.

```
#include <stdio.h>
main()
/*Variable declaration and operations on the variables*
{
int days = 31;
int week = 20;
int month ;
```

```c
if( day== week )
{
printf("First Line - day is equal to week\n" );
}
Else
/*This evaluate the first condition*/
{
printf("First Line - day is not equal to week\n" );
}
if ( day < week )
{
printf("Second Line - day is less than week\n" );
}
else
{
printf("Second Line - day is not less than week\n" );
}
if ( day > week )
{
printf("Third Line - day is greater than week\n" );
}
else
{
printf("Third Line - day is not greater than week\n" );
}
/* Lets change value of day and week */
day = 5;
week = 20;
if ( day <= week )
{
printf("Fourth Line - day is either less than or equal to week\n" );
```

```
}
if ( day >= week )
{
printf("Fifth Line - y is either greater than or equal to week\n" );
}
}
```

Program output:

```
First Line - day is not equal to week
Second Line - day is not less than week
Third Line  - day is greater than week
Fourth Line - day is either less than or equal to week
Fifth Line  - day is either greater than or equal to week
```

Logical Operators in C Programming Language

There are three basic logical operators used in C. The purpose of this operator is to evaluate variables and returns either a 0 or 1 depending on whether an expression is false or true. If you want to write a program that requires making decisions, then you have to use the logical operators.

Operator	Meaning	Example
&&	Logical AND. This operator evaluates	If a =4 and b = 2; the expression

	to true only when both expressions or conditions on the operands are true.	((a==4) && (a<4)) is equivalent to 0.
||	Logical OR. This evaluates to true if one condition operated on the operands is also true.	If a =4 and b = 2; the expression ((a==4) && (a<4)) equals to 1.
!	Logical Not. This returns true only if the operand is 0	If a=5 then, the expression! holds true.

Bitwise Operators

These special operators are used in manipulating data at the bit level. It is used to shift bits from the right position to the left. Nevertheless, they don't work with double float variables.

Bitwise Operator	Meaning
|	OR
^	Exclusive OR
&	AND
<<	Left Shift
>>	Right Shift

Truth Table for bitwise operator

Y	Z	Y ^ Z	Y | Z	Y & Z
0	1	1	1	0
1	0	1	1	0
0	0	0	0	0
1	1	0	1	1

The table above to explain the bitwise operator will make no sense if you are a beginner; the following explanation will clarify it for you. For instance, Y = 60 and Z = 13, the binary format of Y and Z will be 0011 1100 and 0000 1101 respectively

Y = 0011 1100

Z = 0000 1101

From the truth table,

Y | Z = 0011 1101

Y&Z = 0000 1100

Y ^ Z = 0011 0001

I know you may be thinking about how we came about the values below; well it is very simple to understand. Using the Y & Z as an example, the value for Y is 0011 1100 while that of Z is 0000 1101. From the truth table, we go under the Y & Z section. When Y is 0 and Z is 1, what is the value under Y & Z (What you are doing is matching the first binary number of Y with that of Z? obviously, you get a 0. If you continue with that patter, you will get 0000 1100 for Y & Z.

Assignment Operators

The table below will give a better view of what assignment operators work in C programming.

Assignment Operators	Meaning	Example
=	This allocates the value of the right operand to left operand	V = B + D In his situation, the value of B + D will be assigned to V
*=	The left operand gets multiplied by the right operand. furthermore, the product is then allocated to the left operand.	V* = B is equal to V= V*B
-=	This deducts the value of operand on the right from the left before assigning	V -=B This is equivalent to V=V-B

	it to the left.	
+=	This adds the value of the right operand from the left before allocating the value to the content on the left	V+= is equivalent to V=V+B
/=	In this, the value of the operand on the left is divided by the right before assigned to the left	V/= is equivalent to V = V /D

Decision Making in C

It is hard to write a complete program without using decision in C language. What do you think decision-making involves in the context of programming? Well, it is a way of executing certain statements as long as they meet the laid down conditions. However, you will learn the statement, format, and an example to explain the decisions. The diagram below shows a typical decision-making process in C.

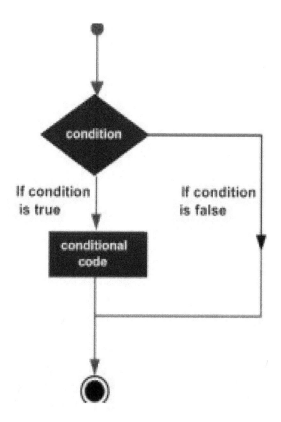

If Statement

This mentions a particular condition and specifies a particular thing will happen if the stated condition or statement becomes true. However, if the condition doesn't turn out true, then the thing suggests will not happen.

Format:

```
if (boolean_condition){
```

/* expression (s) that will perform the action if the Boolean condition stated is true */

}

Diagrammatic representation

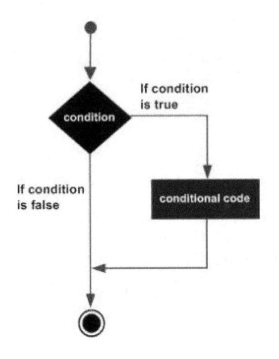

Program to exemplify the "If Statement"

```
#include <stdio.h>
/* Beginning of the main program*/
int main ()
```

```
{
/* Definition of local variables in the program */
int x = 15;
/* Evaluates the boolean condition */
if( y < 30 )
{
/* if the condition (y < 30) is true then display the outcome */
printf("y is less than 30\n" );
}
printf("value of y is : %d\n", a);
return 0;
}
```

Once you finish and the program is executed, your output will look like this:

```
x is less than
```

If ... else Statement

This decision making statement uses an If, which is accompanied by an optional statement that performs the action when the "IF" condition turns false.

Format:

```
if(expression or condition){
```

/* this statement here will be executed as far as the condition is met */
}
Else{
/* expression (s) will be implement if the expression is not true */
}

Diagrammatic Representation

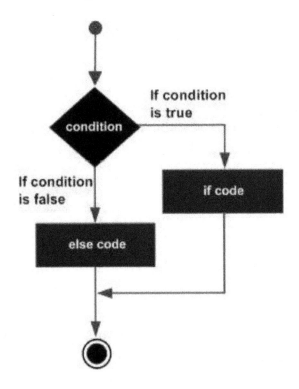

Sample Program for If...else Statement

```
#include <stdio.h>
/* beginning of the execution of the program*/
int main ()
{
/* definition of local variable */
int length = 200;
/* Evaluates the expression or statement*/
if( length< 40 )
{
/* if the expression or statement is true then display the output
as stated */
printf("length is less than 40\n" );
}
else
{
/* if  the condition is not true (false) then display the output as
stated */
printf("length is not less than 40\n" );
}
printf("value of length is : %d\n", length);
return 0;
}
```

Output:

```
length is not less than 40;
```

value of length is: 200

If...else if...else statement

This decision is similar to a situation where you have to make a decision after another decision.

Format:

```
if(Statement1)
{/* if statement1 is evaluated as true, then evaluate the statement */}
else if( statement 2)
{ /* Evaluates statement when statement 2 is true */}
else if( statement 3)
{/* Evaluate when statement 3 is true */}
clsc
{/* Evaluate all conditions are false */}
```

Let's consider a program

```
#include <stdio.h>
int main ()
/* Program execution starts here*/
{
/* Definition of variable */
int x = 90;
```

```c
/* verify the expression */
if( x == 9 )
{
/* if the expression above is true then print what is requested */
printf("Value of x is 9\n" );
}
else if( x == 15 )
{
/* if else if condition is true */
printf("Value of x is 15\n" );
}
else if( x == 60 )
{
}
else
{
/* if none of the conditions is true */
printf("The values don't match\n" );
}
printf("The Precise value of x is: %d\n", x );
return 0;
}
```

Once executed, the output is:

```
The values don't match
```

```
The Precise value of x is: 90
```

Conclusion

The c programming language is not a hard language to learn because it is fundamental for any beginner. If you have completed reading this chapter, I can guarantee that you have the basic knowledge of C programming. However, it is important to dive deeper if you want to perfect your skill with this language.

Chapter Three: C# Programming

Introduction

Did you know that C# is an object-oriented language? Actually, Microsoft developed the language as part of its inbuilt .NET initiative. This programming guide on C# will take you through the basics of C# while equipping you with every concept, you need to understand and relevant programs to explain the language better.

Prerequisite for Learning C#

While there is no standard prerequisite when it comes to learning C#, it is important that as a beginner you have a basic knowledge of computer and programming. However, if you already have previous knowledge on C or C++ language, it will be great. Importantly, before beginning, you have to install Visual Studio. If you are considering space in your system and looking for a way to overcome the hassles of installing the Visual Studio IDE, why not opt to use online compilers.

Features of C# Language

While C# is narrowly similar to various high-level languages such as C and C++ with strong resemblance with Java, however, it does still have a strong programming feature that makes it popular among many programmers in the world. The features include:

- Integration with Windows
- Indexers
- Simple multithreading
- Standard library
- Boolean conditions
- Easy to use generics
- Properties and events
- Assembly versioning
- Automatic garbage collection

Understanding the Basics of C#

To begin, let us start with the simplest program you will come across in any programming language. Yes, it's the simple "Hello World!" program. This involves displaying some text directly to the output screen. The primary aim of this program is to familiarize you with the requirement and syntax of C#.

```
// Hello World! Beginners' Program
namespace Hello
{
  class World {
    static void Main(string[] args)
    {
        System.Console.WriteLine("Hello World, Welcome to My First
```

```
C# Programming!");
    }
  }
}
```

Output

```
Hello World, Welcome to My First C# Programming!
```

Explanation of the Hello World program

// Hello World! Program

Whenever you see a line beginning with "//", it indicates the starting point of a comment in C#. These comments are exempted when the compiler executes the codes in the program. The purpose of comments is to make developers have a better understanding of their codes.

namespace Hello{...}

This line uses the keyword "namespace" to define our own unique namespace. In the example above, our namespace is Hello. Perhaps, it looks abstract. Well, consider namespace as a container that comprises of methods, classes, and other namespace.

class World{...}

The statement above creates a new class "World." Creating a class is compulsory in C# because the language is object-oriented.

static void Main(string[] args){...}

This line must be included in every single program. Main() is a method of class World. The program begins execution from the beginning of the Main() method. Therefore, all programs in C# must contain have a Main() method.

System.Console.WriteLine("Hello World Welcome to C# Programming Language!");

This prints the word in quotes to the screen.

Points to remember

- There must be a class definition for every C# program
- Execution of the program begins from the Main() method
- Comments are not compulsory but necessary

The program above is an introduction for beginners. Later in this chapter, you will see other programs that may seem complex. However, the secret is compiling them on your own while making some changes. If nothing makes sense so far, don't worry with time, everything will be clearer.

Data types

Nothing should be new to you at this point, because some of these terms have been explained in previous chapters. However, it is important to throw more light on them once a while. The C# language has its own basic data types, which we will discuss in this section. You can use data types in C# to build values that will be used in the course of the program or application. Let us expound on these data types with example.

Integer

Integer data types work with numbers, which are normally whole numbers. C# uses the reserves word "Int32" to declare a variable as an integer type. For instance, if I declare the variable number1 as an integer. After this, I will further allocate a numerical value to number1

```
using System;
namespace DemoProgram
{
 class Program
//This part creates a new class, which we call Program
 {
  static void Main(string[] args)
  {
   Int32 number1=50;
   Console.Write(number1);

   Console.ReadKey();
  }
 }
}
```

The outcome of the program above will be:

50

Explanation: We declare the variable "number1" to be of integer type (Int32) with the value "50" assigned to the variable. Then the result is displayed to the console.

Double

This data type is used when decimal numbers are involved. Examples include 10.58, 25.98, or 45.01. In C#, the keyword "Double" is used to denote a double data type. In the example below, the variable "number1" is defined as double and a value assigned to it.

```
using System;
namespace DemoProgram
{
 class Program
// This part creates a new class, which we call Program
 {
  static void Main(string[] args)
  {
// Declaration of the variable "number" to be of double data type
   double number1=45.01;
   Console.Write(num);

   Console.ReadKey();
  }
```

```
  }
}
```

The output of the program will display

45.01

Boolean

The Boolean data type works with Boolean values, which can only be false or true. The keyword "Boolean" is used to declare this kind of datatype. For instance, the program below declares "OFF" as Boolean with the value "False" assigned to it. Eventually, the console display "False" as the output.

```
using System;
namespace DemoProgram
{
 class Program
// We create a new class call Program
 {
   static void Main(string[] args)
   {
// Here is the declaration of the variables as Boolean
    Boolean OFF=false;
    Console.Write(status);

    Console.ReadKey();
   }
```

```
 }
}
```

String

At times, when writing a program, you may choose to write a specific message shown on the screen. To do this, the "string" data type allows text to be displayed. It uses the keyword "String"

```
using System;
namespace DemoProgram
// The goal of this program is to display a string on the screen
{
 class program
// We create a new class called Program
 {
  static void Main(string[] args)
  {
  String statement1="This is C# Programming for Beginners'.";
  Console.Write(statement1);

  Console.ReadKey();
 }
 }
}
```

The output will be:

This is C# Programming for Beginners'.

Variables

In C#, it is a memory location that contains a data type that determines the kind of value to store in the variable. Variables are declared in the format below:

[modifiers] data type identifier;

The modifier in the format above represents an access modifier. On the other hand, the identifier represents the variable name. The first example below shows a variable declaration where the public is the modifier, number1 is an identifier name, and int is the data type. However, the second example indicates that the second variable type is a local variable.

Public int number1; // First example

Int number1; // second example

Variable Modifiers

A modifier allows a programmer to specify some features, which is applied to the identifier. A local variable has a scope, which is defined within the block in the program.

Modifier	Meaning
Internal	Accessible only by the current

	program
Public	Accessible as a field anywhere in the program
Protected	Accessible within the class it is defined
Private	Accessible within the type in which it is defined

Constants

Constants are values whose values don't change throughout the program time frame. C# uses the keyword "const" and it always comes before the data type and variable. If you decide to allocate value to a particular constant, it will return compilation error. For instance,

const int number1 = 45;

number1 = 89;

// This will be a compilation error because the assignment towards the left side has to be an indexer, variable or property.

Note that local variables can be declared as constants. These constants are usually static, even if they don't use any static keyword.

Operators in C#

You should be familiar with operators even if you are a beginner. These are symbols used in programming to perform various operations on an operand. Operands can be either constants or variables. For instance, in 3 * 6, * is an operation used to perform multiplication operation whereas 3 and 6 are the operands. You can use operators in C# to manipulate values and variables in the course of a program. However, C# supports numerous operators depending on the operation type they perform. Without much time, let us begin with the operators in C#.

Arithmetic Operators

These operators are used for various numeric data types, which includes arithmetic operations including addition (+), subtraction (-), multiplication (*), and division (/). Furthermore, C# has another unique arithmetic operator known as the %, which is the remainder after a division operation is performed.

Importantly, unlike other languages, the operator + (addition) operate differently when used with string and number types. For instance, the result of the expression 7 + 4 is 11. However, when used with strings, the result of the expression, "7 +4" is "74". Therefore, with the number type, it acts as an addition whereas with strings, it is a concatenation operator. A simple program can be helpful to set things in order.

```csharp
using System;

namespace Oper
{
        class ArithmeticOper
        {
// Always remember you have to create a new class by using the class
statement
                public static void Main(string[] args)
                {
                        double income = 12.20, expenses = 2.30, res;
                        int loss = 21, profit = 4, ; dem
                        // Addition operator (+)
                        res = income + expenses;
                        Console.WriteLine("{0} + {1} = {2}", income,
expenses, res);


                        res = income - expenses;
                        Console.WriteLine("{0} - {1} = {2}", income,
expenses, res);


                        res = income * expenses;
                        Console.WriteLine("{0} * {1} = {2}", income,
expenses, res);
```

```
12.2 + 2.3 = 14.5
12.2 − 2.3 = 9.9
```

```
                    res = income / expenses;
                    Console.WriteLine("{0} / {1} = {2}", income,
expenses, res);


                    dem = loss % profit;
                    Console.WriteLine("{0} % {1} = {2}", loss, profit,
dem);
                }
        }
}
```

When you properly compile this program without any error, you will get the following output.

```
12.2 * 2.3 = 28.06
12.2 / 2.3 = 5.30434782609
21 % 4 = 1
```

Logical Operators

You can use these operators to perform logical operations and they include AND, OR. These operators operate on Boolean expression and return the same Boolean values. The result can only be true (T) or false (F) as illustrated in the table below.

Operand Y	Operand Z	AND (&&)	OR (||)
T	T	T	T
F	T	F	T
T	F	F	T
F	F	F	F

From the table, the OR operator evaluates to true (T) only in a situation where one operand is true (T). However, for the AND operator, once one operand is false (F), the operation is also False.

Sample program

```
using System;
```

```
namespace Operator
{
        class Logical
// Here, we name the class we created as Operator
        {
                public static void Main(string[] args)
                {
// Declaration and giving variables values
                        bool outcome;
                        int income = 20, expenses = 30;
                        // OR operator
                        outcome = (income == expenses) || (income> 5);
                        Console.WriteLine(outcome);
                        // AND operator
                        outcome = (income == expenses) && (incomeb >
5);
                        Console.WriteLine(outcome);
                }
        }
}
```

The outcome of the program above should be:

True

False

Note: These programs are for explanatory purposes. It is important for you to try it on your own. If you want to learn to program effectively, you must be ready to practice frequently and this is a way to improve your programming skill.

Relational Operators

These operators in C# return either a true or a false result. If you want to compare variables or expression, the best option is the relational operator. Additionally, they have a lower priority in comparison with arithmetic operators. Besides this, you can use them in loop and decision-making. The table below shows the basic relational operators in C#.

Relational Operators	Name of Operator	Example
==	Equal to	6 == 7 return false
!=	Not equal to	5 != 7 return true
>	Greater than	7 > 5 returns true
<	Less than	8 < 9 evaluates true
<=	Less than or (equivalent) equal to	9<= 7 evaluates true
>=	Greater than or equal to	5 >= 7 returns false

Sample Program

```csharp
using System;

namespace Oper
{
        class Relational
        {
                public static void Main(string[] args)
                {
// Declaration of variables
                        int outcome;
                        int day1 = 21, day3 = 23;
                        outcome = (day1==day3);
                        Console.WriteLine("{0} == {1} returns {2}",day1,
day3, outcome);

                        outcome= (day1 > day3);
                        Console.WriteLine("{0} > {1} returns {2}",day1,
day3, outcome);

                        outcome = (day1< day3);
                        Console.WriteLine("{0} < {1} returns {2}",day1,
day3, outcome);

                        outcome = (day1 >= day3);
                        Console.WriteLine("{0} >= {1} returns {2}",day1,
day3, outcome);

                        outcome = (day1 <= day3);
                        Console.WriteLine("{0} <= {1} returns {2}",day1,
day3, outcome);

                        outcome = (day1 != day3);
                        Console.WriteLine("{0} != {1} returns {2}",day1,
```

```
day3, outcome);
            }
        }
}
```

Output:

```
20 == 30 returns False
20 > 30 returns False
20 < 30 returns True
20 >= 30 returns False
20 <= 30 returns True
20 != 30 returns True
```

Unary Operators

These operators unlike the ones we have discussed so far operate on one operand instead of both. The unary operators in C# include

Operator	Name	Description
-	Unary Minus	Inverts the operand sign
+	Unary Plus	Leaves the operand to sign the way it is
--	Decrement	Decreases value by 1
++	Increment	Increase value by 1

Sample Program for Unary Operator

```
using System;

namespace UnaryOperator
{
    class UnaryOpe
    {
        public static void Main(string[] args)
        {
// Declaration of variables in the program
            int num = 25, outcome;
            bool flag = false;
            outcome = +num;
            Console.WriteLine("+num = " + outcome);
            outcome = -num;
            Console.WriteLine("-num = " + outcome);
            outcome = ++num;
            Console.WriteLine("++num = " + outcome);
            outcome = --num;
            Console.WriteLine("--num = " + outcome);
            Console.WriteLine("!flag = " + (!flag));
        }
    }
}
```

The output is as follows:

```
+num = 25
-num = -25
++number = 26
--number = 25
!flag = True
```

Bitwise Operators

In our last operators in C# is the bitwise operator, which performs bit manipulation similar to what I have explained in the preceding chapter. Since you are familiar with the operation, I will simply highlight the operators and a simple program to demonstrate how they work. For more, you can check "Chapter Two" to refresh your memory.

Operator	Operator Name (Bitwise)
&	AND
^	Exclusive OR
|	OR
~	Complement
<<	Left Shift
>>	Right Shift

Look at the program below.

```
using System;

namespace OperBit
{
// Creating a new class known as BitOpe
        class BitOpe
        {

                public static void Main(string[] args)
                {
// Declaration of variables with values
                        int income = 20;
                        int expenses = 30;
                        int outcome;
                        outcome = ~income;
                        Console.WriteLine("~{0} = {1}", income,
outcome);

                        outcome = income&expenses;
                        Console.WriteLine("{0} & {1} = {2}",
income,expenses, outcome);
                        outcome = income | expenses;
                        Console.WriteLine("{0} | {1} = {2}",
income,expenses, outcome);
                        outcome = income ^ expenses;
                        Console.WriteLine("{0} ^ {1} = {2}",
income,expenses, outcome);
```

```
                         outcome = income<< 2;
                         Console.WriteLine("{0} << 2 = {1}", income,
outcome);

                         outcome = income>> 2;
                         Console.WriteLine("{0} >> 2 = {1}", income,
outcome);
                }
        }
}
```

If the program doesn't contain any error, your output should be as follows:

```
~20 = -21
20 & 30 = 0
20 | 30 = 50
20 ^ 30 = 50
20 << 2 = 40
20 >> 2 = 2
```

Ternary Operator

This operator will be strange because it is the first time I am mentioning it in this book. The ternary operator "?" operates on three operands and functions like the "if... then... else" statement.

Format:

Variable = condition? Statement1: statement2;

The operation works this way. If the condition stated is true, then the outcome of statment1 is allocated to the variable. However, if it turns out to be false, the value is allocated to statement2. Consider the program below.

```
using System;

namespace OperTer
{
        class Ternary
// The new class name for this program is Ternary
        {
                public static void Main(string[] args)
                {
// Declaration of variables as integer and string
                        int num = 21;
                        string outcome;
                        outcome = (num % 2 == 0)? "Even Number" :
"Odd Number";
                        Console.WriteLine("{0} is {1}", num, outcome);
                }
        }
}
```

The output will be:

With this, I believe you have an excellent understanding of operators in C#. You are surely making progress in your quest to be an around programmer.

Array

An array in C# is simply a data structure, which stores a group or sequence of fixed-size elements. All elements have the same size. In a simple way, it is a storage position for a sequence of data, which is considered as a group or collection of variables having a similar data type.

For instance, you intend to have array but with an integer value, you have to first declare it.

Int [5];

In the example above, the total number of elements will be 5 i. An array is very efficient, especially when you need to store a group of values with a similar data type. Therefore, rather than declaring the variable one after the other, you can decide to use one declaration for them all. The variable will reference the list of array elements in the program. An example will make things easier for you.

```
namespace demoProgram {
   class programArray
{
// Study the program carefully how the array is declared
   Static void main (string[] args)
 Int [] Table;
    }
   }
}
```

In the example above, you have an idea of the line – Int [] numbers;

So far, you should know that we are using an integer data type. The [] is the placeholder, which specifies the array rank. It identifies the exact number of elements contained in that array we want. Lastly, the array has a name, which in this example is "Table"

Let's go further with this example, consider the next line of codes.

```
using System;

namespace demoApplication {
```

```
    class ArrayProgram
{

  Static void main (string[] args)
 Int [] Table;
  Table = new Int [5];
  Table [0] = 8;
  Table [1] = 9;
  Table [2] = 10;
  Table [3] = 11;
  Table [4] = 12;
  Table [5] = 13
    }
  }
}
```

What we did here is to initialize the array by specifying the number of "Table" the array will accommodate. Furthermore, I assigned values to each array element. In array, the index position always begins at 0.

Let us assume you want to display the full content of the program. It will look like this.

```
namespace DemoApplication
{
 class ArrayProgram
 {
  static void Main(string[] args)
// Declaration of variables begins here
  {
   Int[] Table;
   Table=new Int[3];

Table [0] = 8;
   Table [1] =9;
   Table [2] = 10;
   Table [3] = 11;
   Table [4] = 12;
   Table [5] = 13;

   Console.WriteLine(Table[0]);
   Console.WriteLine(Table[1]);
   Console.WriteLine(Table[2]);
   Console.WriteLine(Table[3]);
   Console.WriteLine(Table[4]);
   Console.WriteLine(Table[5]);

   Console.ReadKey();
  }
 }
```

```
}
```

In C# programming language, you can declare the array as fixed or dynamic length. For the static length, you can store array on a pre-defined number of items as shown in our examples above. However, a dynamic array doesn't have predefined size rather the size increases as new items are added. It is also possible to alter a dynamic array after defining it.

Arrays Definition for Different Data Type

In our previous examples, all the arrays are of integer type. However, it is not limited to an integer data type as you can use various data types including string, character, and double. Importantly, arrays are objects in C# language. This signifies that after the declaration of the array, it doesn't mean that the array is now created. You have to instantiate the array through the "new" operator.

Check out the examples below to know how to define arrays of string, char, and double.

```
using System;

namespace demoProgram {
    class program
```

```
// Beginning of the program
{
    Static void main (string[] args)
// Declaration of elements in the array
 string [] stringArray = new string [20];
 bool [] boolArray = new bool [2];
 char [] charArray = new char [7];
 double [] doubleArray = new double [4];
    }
  }
}
```

Categories of Array in C#

You can categorize arrays into four groups. These include single-dimensional arrays, rectangular arrays or multidimensional arrays, jagged, and mixed arrays. My focus will be on the first two arrays because jagged and mixed arrays will be complicated for you to understand as a beginner.

Single-Dimensional

These set of arrays are the simplest and easiest to understand in C#. You can use single-dimensional arrays to store items of an array with an already predefined data type. The items in the array are stored continuously beginning from 0. So far, all the arrays I have explained in this chapter are single-dimensional arrays.

The code below declares and sets an array containing five items, with all having an integer data type. First is to declare the array before instantiating the array using the new operator.

```
int [] numberArray;
numberArray = new int [5];
```

C# uses a straightforward way of declaring arrays by putting the items in curly braces. Note that if a program forgets to initialize the array, the items are inevitably initialized to its definite original value for that array type. The code below should explain it better.

1	int [] staticIntArray = new int [5] {2, 4, 6, 8, 10};
2	string [] strArray = new string [4] {"Johnson", "Mikel, "Frederick", "Mahesh"};
3	string [] strArray = {"Johnson", "Mikel, "Frederick", "Mahesh"};

From the three different codes, you will observe that the first example declares an array with 5 items. The second declares an array with string data type having 4 string items. However, the second and third examples are the same with the only difference being that we directly assigned the values to the array without using the new operator.

Multi-Dimensional

This kind of arrays contains more than one dimension. Most beginners tend to run away from this kind of arrays because they look complex. It has the form of a matrix. This type of array can be of fixed or dynamic size. However, to declare a multi-dimensional array, the format is as follows:

string [,] mutliDimStringArray

Initializing multi-dimensional arrays

The code below shows two different multi-dimensional arrays. It defines an array with a matric of 3x2 and 2x2 respectively. It is possible to store 6 items in the first array while 4 on the second. You should initialize both arrays during declaring it.

```
int[,] Mynumbers = new int[3, 2] { { 4, 2 }, { 5, 2 }, { 1, 3 } };
string[,] names = new string[2, 2] { { "Queen", "Ben" }, { "Paul",
"Irene" } };
```

What if you are unsure the items the array will contain?. The code below clarifies that by creating two-dimensional arrays without any limit to the number of items.

```
int[,] numbers = new int[,] { { 4, 2 }, { 5, 2 }, { 1, 3 } };
string[,] names = new string[,] { { "Queen", "Ben" }, { "Paul",
"Irene" } };
```

Similar to the single-dimensional array where we omit the new operator, you can also do the same in multi-dimensional arrays by directly assigning the values.

```
namespace demoApplication {
    class programArray
{
// Don't forget we always have to create a new class
    Static void main (string[] args)
        int[, ] MyTable = {
        {
            4,
            2
        },
        {
            5,
            2
        },
        {
```

```
        1,
        3
     }
  };
  string[, ] names = {
     {
        "Queen",
        "Ben"
     },
     {
        "Paul",
        "Irene"
     }
  };
     }
  }
}
```

The code above may look complicated but we can make it simpler by initializing the array items one after the order. Look at the code below

```
int [, ] numb = new int [3, 2];
numb [0, 0] = 4;
numb [1, 0] = 2;
numb [2, 0] = 5;
numb [0, 1 ] = 2;
```

```
numb [1, 1] = 1;
numb [2, 1] = 3;
```

To access a multi-dimensional array items, you have to specify the dimension of the matrix. For instance, item (1, 2) exemplifies an array item on the second row and third column of the matrix. For you to access the "numb" array, you have to use the "Console.Writeline"

```
1.      Console.WriteLine(numb[0, 0]);
2.      Console.WriteLine(numb[0, 1]);
3.      Console.WriteLine(numb[1, 0]);
4.      Console.WriteLine(numb[1, 1]);
5.      Console.WriteLine(numb[2, 0]);
6.      Console.WriteLine(numb[2, 2]);
```

Note: You can perform various manipulations on arrays such as sorting, searching, reversing, and clearing an array list. So far, you have learned the basics of arrays including their various types. Don't forget to try some exercises on your own.

Chapter Four: Beginners Guide to Learning C++

Yes, you have graduated after finishing your first course in this "Step by Step Beginners' Guide to Learn Programming" book. If you did go through the C programming language explained in the previous chapter, give yourself a treat because you have accomplished what many cannot do in a lifetime.

Welcome back from your treat. It is time to improve yourself in diversifying your programming skill in key languages. By the time you are through with this chapter, you will be better equipped to write codes using C++ language. In the end, you will roll your sleeve and program like a "badass" programmer.

C++ will help you understand the modern approach to software development. For a new developer, the essential thing is to understand the theories of programming, which will help you by not wasting your precious time with the technical details of the language.

Brief History

In 1979, Bjarne Stroustrup developed C++ Programming language. Originally, the language was known as "C with classes" before the name was changed to C++ in 1983. The name is a demonstration that the language comes from the C programming language. Today, the language has evolved with C++14 as the standard C++. This version comes with added feature including the fixing of some bugs. The introduction of the C++14 took place on March 2014.

Is there anyone using C++?

The language is relevant in various sectors in the software industry. it may surprise you to know that the OS of your favorite Apple laptop is written in C++. Besides it, operating systems such as Windows 95, 98, Me, 2000, and the once-popular Window XP were also written in this language. Applications such as Internet Explorer, Microsoft Office, applications of Adobe Systems (Illustrator, ImageReady, Flash, Photoshop, Acrobat, etc.) are developed using C++. Furthermore, not forgetting the renowned Chromium Web Browser, and Google Search engine, these are just a few to mention.

Why use C++ today?

Today, many software developers use C++ when the application requires efficiency and high performance. This has made many recognize C++ as a flexible and efficient language. Additionally, if you want to develop a big application but want less resource to use, then C++ is the best option.

Difference between C and C++

Hardly can you talk about C++ without considering the difference with C programming language. Most beginners tend to find out what makes these two languages differ. C is a procedural language but doesn't support classes and objects. However, C++ is not only a procedural programming language but also an object-oriented language. There are other differences that exist between these two languages, which are shown below in the tabular form.

Differences	C Programming Language	C++ Programming Language
Developers	AT&T Bell Labs by Dennis Ritchie in 1969	Bjarne Stroustrup in 1979
Division	Subset of C++	Superset of C. This means you can run C programs in C++ environment
Language support	Procedural language	Procedural and Object-oriented language
Multiple Declaration	Multiple global declarations are	Not allowed

	allowed	
Overloading support	Function and operator not supported	Supports operators and function overloading
Reference Variables	Not supported	Supported
Namespace feature	Not available	Available
Inheritance	Not possible	Allowed
Exception handling	Not supported	Supported
Input	Scanf	Cin
Output	Printf	cout

Structure of C++ Program

Since you already have a basic understanding of programming, I will teach you C++ by using a different strategy. Perhaps, the best way to learn any programming language is y writing a program. Does that sound interesting? Of course, I will start with a simple program, which you can modify. If you want to learn to program faster, always experiment with some addition.

From the sample of this program, I will explain the structure of the C++ program. So let us begin with our first C++ program.

`// First Programming in C++`
`#include <iostream>`
`using namespace std;`
`Int main ()`
`{`
`cout <<"Welcome to C++ Programming!";`
`return 0;`
`}`
	Welcome to C++ Programming!

The panel on the left side represents the source code while the right side shows the result of the program after compilation and execution.

// First Programming in C++

Whenever you see a line starting with "//" in the C++ program, it indicates a comment line. They don't have any effect on the course of the program. however, the reason behind them is for the programming to make some observation or explanations. It allows you to make a short description of what the program is all about

#include <iostream>

Lines starting with # are directives for the preprocessor. Although they are not normal code lines with expressions, however, are indications for the compiler's preprocessor. In the program above, the directive tells the preprocessor to add the iostream to the standard file.

Using namespace std;

Every element in the standard C++ library is usually declared in a namespace. Therefore, for one to access its functionality, you must declare use this expression to do that.

Int main ()

This line indicates the beginning of the main function definition. The main function is the starting point of any C++ programs and their execution begins here. For any program, a pair of parentheses () always follow the word "main" What differentiates a function from other types of expression is the parentheses that follow the name.

cout << "Welcome to C++ Programming!";

This line is a C++ statement. The cout is a standard output stream in C++, which is followed by a sequence of characters enclosed in quotes. If you observe clearly, the statement ends with a semicolon (;).

Return o;

The return statement makes the main function (int main ()) to terminate.

Data Types, Variables and Operator

Perhaps, you will question the usefulness of the program above. We had to write some lines containing statements, compile and execute them to produce a simple output on the screen. Why even compile it when you can produce it quickly without having to run the program. Interestingly, C++ programming is not limited to printing text on the screen. You can perform other activities. In this section, I will introduce you to the concept of variables, data types, and operators in C++ language.

Assuming I ask you to store the number 9 in your memory. After a while, I ask you to memorize any number 8. With this, you have to store two different numbers in your memory. Let us assume that I ask you to add 3 to the first number I asked you to store. For now, you have to retain a new number, which is 10 (9 +1) in addition to the second number 3. Furthermore, subtract the first number from the second, which will be 7.

This whole process you have just completing using your memory is similar to what a computer with two variables. The same action can be executed using the following

instruction.

```
A = 9;
B = 3;
A = a+1;
Result = a – b;
```

This is very simple, right. Assuming you have to store millions of numbers, can your brain accommodate it? Emphatically, No! However, a computer can store much more than that and perform sophisticated mathematical operations. A Variable is part of a memory that stores a determined value.

Every variable requires an identifier, which differentiates it from others. For instance, in the example above, the variable identifiers include a, b, and results. You can call the variable any name you like.

Identifiers

An identifier is valid if it has a sequence of one or more letters, underscore character (_), or digits. However, there shouldn't be any symbols, punctuation marks or space when naming an identifier. The only valid characters are letters, digits and underscore. Additionally, every variable identifier must start with a letter. Besides this, you can also use an underscore; however, in certain situations, they are reserved as specific keywords.

When naming an identifier, another important thing to consider is that they should not be keywords. Keywords are specific words used only by the compiler.

The standard reserved keywords in C++ language include asm, auto, bool, break, case, catch, char, class, const, const_cst, continue, default, delete, do, double, dynamic_cast, else, enum, explicit, export extern, false, float, for, friend, goto, if, inline, int, ling, mutable, namespace, new, operator, private, protected, public, register, reinterpret_cast, return, short, signed, sizeof, static, static_cast, struct, switch, template, this, throw, true, try, typedef, typeid, typename, union, unsigned, using, virtual, void, volatile, wchar_t, while

Note – Like C language, the C++ language is case sensitive. This means that when you write an identifier in capital letters, it is not equivalent to another having the same name in small letters. For instance, the variable HOUSE is not the same as using "house" or "House" as a variable. The three examples are different identifiers.

Data Types in C++ Programming Language

In programming, variables are stored in computer memory; however, the computer must know the particular data you want it to store because it is not going to be the same amount of memory using in storing a letter or a number. Besides this, they are not interpreted in the same way.

Memory is organized in bytes. A byte is the smallest amount of memory, which can be managed in C++. The table below highlights the basic data types available in C++ along with their size and range.

Data Type	Description	Size (byte) *	Range *
Char	Character	1	-128 to 127 and 0 – 255
Short int	Short integer	2	-32768 to 32767 for signed while unsigned is 0 to 65535
Int	Integer	4	-2147483648 to 2147483647 for signed while unsigned is 0 to 4294967295
Long int	Long integer	4	Signed - 2147483648 to 2147483647 while unsigned

			is 0 to 4294967295
Float	Floating point number	4	+/- 3.4e +/-38
Bool	Boolean value	1	True or false
Double	Double precision floating point number	8	+/- 1.7e +/- 308
Long double	Long double-precision floating-point number	8	/- 1.7e +/- 308
Wchar_t	Wide character	2 or 4	1 wide character

** The values of the size and range of the data types depends on the preprocessor of the system that the program is compiled. However, the above table shows the values for a 32-bit system.

Variable Declaration

You cannot use a variable in C++ unless you declare it. When you hear of variable declaration, it means stating the particular data type you want that variable to be. the syntax for variable declaration involves writing the particular data type and followed by a valid variable identifier. You must adhere to the rule of variable number in order not to have issues when writing your program.

For instance

```
Int abe;
Float newNumber;
```

In C++, these two are valid variables declared. The first one declares "ab" as a variable of integer type while the second declares the word "newNumber" as a variable type of float. Once these variables have been declared, you can use them within the program. however, instead of declaring a different variable of the same type on different lines, you can decide to put them on the same line and separate them using a comma.

For example, if you were to declare a, b, c, d, and e as an integer, you can declare them like this:

Int a, b, c;

Rather than

Int a;

Int b;

Int c;

Since you are new to the language, I will use an example to demonstrate with a variable declaration in a program.

```
// Declaring Variable
#include <iostream>
using namespace std;
int main ()
{
int A, B;
int Outcome;

// The Process of Variable declaration
A = 5;
B = 14;
A = A + 1;
Outcome = A * B;
// Print the outcome of the process
cout << Outcome;
// End the Program
Return 0;
}
```

Output

84

Is there anything looking strange in the above program? Obviously, it shouldn't because we have covered most of the areas in the program. However, the only line that may look strange is the "A = A +1; else everything looks good.

Variable Scope

A variable in C++ can be in a global or local scope. When you declare a variable within the body of the source code is it global; nevertheless, a local variable is one declared within the body of a block or function. If you look at our program above, you will observe that the variables were declared along with the data type was declared at the beginning of the main function (int main ()). Global variables can be referenced from anywhere in the program, it does not matter if it is inside a function. However, local variables are limited to enclosed braces {}. The diagram below is self-explanatory for you.

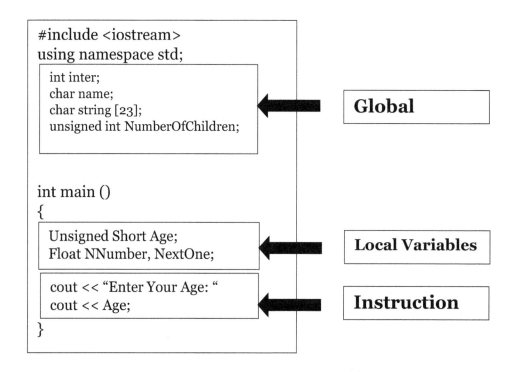

```
#include <iostream>
using namespace std;
    int inter;
    char name;
    char string [23];
    unsigned int NumberOfChildren;


int main ()
{
    Unsigned Short Age;
    Float NNumber, NextOne;

    cout << "Enter Your Age: "
    cout << Age;
}
```

Global

Local Variables

Instruction

Variable Initialization

When you declare local variables, by default its value is undetermined. However, you may decide to store a value when you are declaring the variable. For this to happen, you would have to initialize the variable. There are two ways of variable initialization in C++.

The first one involves appending and equal sign (=) followed by the value, which the variable will initialize. For instance, I want to declare a variable "A" of data type integer while initializing it to the value 5 at the moment. This will be:

Int A = 5;

The second means of initializing variables is through a process called "constructor initialization", which involves enclosing the initial value between parentheses (()). For instance,

Int A (0);

In C++, both ways of variable initialization are valid and acceptable.

``// Variable Initialization in C++
#include <iostream>
using namespace std;
int main ()
{
int A, B;
int Outcome;
 	
// The Process of Variable declaration
A = 5;   //initial value = 5
B (14); // initial value = 14
A = A + 1;
result = A * B;
// Print the outcome of the process
cout << result;
// End the Program
Return 0;
}```
	84

Strings in C++ Programming

Variables with non-numerical value and longer than a single character are known as a string. The C++ has its own standard library that allows strings operation. Although it is not a fundamental data type, it does behave in a similar fashion as data types.

To be able to use a string in C++, you have to include an additional header in your program.

```
// String Operation in C++
#include <iostream>
#include <string>
using namespace std;
int main ()
{
string myName = "My Name is
Johnbull Cosmos.";
cout << myName;

Return 0;
}
```

My Name is Johnbull Cosmos.

This is quite enough to understand string, as I will not dive deep into its operation. With this, you can display a string with various characters. Remember, you have to declare the variable with the string keyword (string myName = "My Name is Johnbull Cosmos.";)

Constants

By now you will understand what constants or literals are if you go through the C programming in chapter two. It has the same operation in C++; constants are used to express the value of a variable in the course of the program. Remember our previous program where we declare A = 5. In this situation, 5 is a literal constant. Literal constants are categorized as follows

Integer numerals

These numerical constant specify integer decimal values. To use a numerical constant you don't require any special character or quote attached to them. Examples of integer numerals include

1176

45

-404

Floating-point number

These numbers have decimal or exponents. They include a decimal point or e character or both attached together. For instance,

3.1578

2.25e23

16.5e-19

Character and string Constant

At times, you may have non-numerical constants such as:

'e'

'Hello World'

'My C++ Programming Lesson'

Defining Constant in C++

You may decide to define your own constant in the course of a process without having to consume memory. You can do this by using the #define preprocessor directive. The format is as follow

#define variable value

For example:

 #define Pi = 3.142

#define newline '\'

From the example above, the #define defines two new constants with variable name Pi and newline.

```
// Example for Defining Constants in C++
#include <iostream>
using namespace std;
#define Pi = 3.142
#define newline '\n'

int main ()
{
double r = 9.0
double circle;
circle = 2 * Pi * r;
cout << circle;
cout << newline;
Return 0;
}
```

56.556

Operators in C++ Programming Language

Now you have the basic knowledge of data types, variables, and constants, it is time to start operating with them. C++ has its own integrated operators to perform such activity. Most programming languages have their operators as keywords but in C++, you can use your normal signs on the keyboard. It depends on English words to perform various operations. Additionally, you don't have to memorize anything in this section.

C++ offers various types of operators to use with literals and variables to get a result. Perhaps you know the basic operators from your C programming section. However, there are other operators that C++ language has. I will take them one after another while using examples to explain how they work.

Arithmetic Operators

I don't have to explain much about this operator since you already know them. However, the basic arithmetic operators in C++ include +, -, *, /, and % (modulo). Modulo is the remainder when you divide two numbers. For instance, in a program, you wrote

```
b = 21 % 5;
```

The variable b will contain 1 since that is the remainder when you divide 21 between 5.

Besides this, there are two additional operators known as the decrement (--) and increment operators (++). These two operators can be used before (prefix) or after (postfix or suffix) a variable. In as much as expressions such as b++ and ++b have the same meaning; however, in a situation where the result of the decrease or increase is evaluated in as a value in an outer expression, the meaning will be different. In the scenario where the increment operator is the prefix (++b), the value of the variable "b" is increased before you evaluate the result of the expression

On the other hand, where the increment operator is the postfix (b++) the value of the variable "b" is increased after the evaluation of the operation. Does it sound confusing? Well, an example will make it clearer for you.

Example 1	Example 2
B=4; C = ++B; //A contains 4 while B contains 4	B=4; C=++B //C contains 3 while B contains 4

Does it make any sense now? Of course, it should be if you are not clear, here is the explanation.

In the first example, the content of B is first increased before the value is copied to A whereas in the second example, the value of B is copied A before the value of B is increased.

Study the Program below, what do you think will be the output?

```
int main()
{
        int i = 0;
        while(i < 10)
```

```
    {
        cout << i++; //post increment
    }
    cout << endl;
    i = 0;
    while(i<10)
    {
        cout << ++i; //pre increment
    }
    return 0;
}
```

Logical Operators

There are three logical operators in C++, which are the conjunction (&&), disjunction (||), and the negation (!) operators. You can also refer to them as the AND, OR, and NOT operator.

The table below shows the AND and OR logical operators

A	B	A&&B	A||B
True	True	True	True
True	False	False	True

False	True	False	True
False	False	False	False

Table for NOT

Logical Operator	NOT
True	False
False	True

Relational Operators

The relational operator is used to evaluate a comparison between two values or expression. The result of the relational operation is normally a Boolean value, which can only be true or false (0 for true and 1 for false). The format is as follows:

Operand1 (operational operator) operand2

The operands can be a literal or a variable. The following are the relational operators in C++

Relational Operators	Description	Meaning
==	Equal to	Returns true if both operand 1 and 2 are equal
!=	Not Equal to	Returns true if both operands are not equal

>	Greater than	Returns true if operand 1 is greater than operand 2
<	Less than	Returns true if operand 1 is less than operand 2
>=	Greater than or equal to	Returns true if operand 1 is greater than or equal to operand two, else it is false
<=	Less than or equal to	Returns true if operand 1 is less than or equal to operand two, else it is false

Example of Relational Operators

```
// Example of Relational Operators
#include <iostream>
using namespace std;
int main ()
```

```
{
int four = 4;
int six = 6;
cout << " 4 is equal to 6 = " << (four == six) << endl;
cout << " 4 is not equal to 6 = " << (four != six) << endl;
cout << " 4 is less than 6 = " << (four < six) << endl;
cout << " 4 is greater than 6 = " << (four > six) << endl;
cout << " 4 is not less than 6 = " << (four >= six) << endl;
cout << " 4 is not greater than  = " << (four <= six) << endl;
   return 0;
}
```

If you compile and execute this program properly, you will see the output as:

```
4 is equal to 6 = 0
4 is not equal to 6 = 1
4 is less than 6 = 1
4 is greater than 6 = 0
4 is not less than 6 = 0
4 is not greater than 6 = 1
```

Bitwise Operators

This operator is similar to the logical operators we just discussed. However, it performs logical operations on bits. Unlike the logical operators, that use true or false, the bitwise operators return the output as either 0 or 1.

Operator	ASM Equivalent	Description
&	AND	Bitwise AND
^	XOR	Bitwise Exclusive OR
|	OR	Bitwise Inclusive OR

A	B	A & B	A | B	A ^ B
0	0	0	0	0
0	1	0	1	1
1	1	1	1	0
1	0	0	1	1

Now, are you wondering how come about the 1's and the 0's? I didn't perform any magic here. Here is the secret. For the bitwise "&", the bit is 1 only when both variables (A and B) have 1 as their corresponding bit. For the XOR, the resulting bit is 1f only one variable has the corresponding bit whereas the OR must have at least a variable with 1 in its corresponding bit.

111

Assignment Operators

The function of this operator is to assign a value on the right-hand side to the variable on the left. It uses the "=" as the operator in C++. You can also combine assignment operators with the different operators mentioned so far in this chapter. If you combine them, they form a composite or compound assignment operator. Composite operators include +=, -=, *=, /=, >>=, <<=, %=, |=, ^=, and &=.

Consider the following expression

Expression	Meaning
Number1 += number2;	Number1 = Number1 + number2;
b-= 10;	b = b − 10;
cost *= profit + 2;	cost = cost * (profit +1);

Example of all Composite Assignment operators

Let A = 20 initially for the below examples

Composite Assignment Operator	Example	Is Equivalent to	Result
+=	A += 2	A = A + 2	22
-=	A -= 2	A = A - 2	8

*=	A *= 2	A = A * 2	20
/=	A /= 2	A = A / 2	5
%=	A%= 2	A = A % 2	0
<<=	A <<= 2	A = A << 2	40
>>=	A >>= 2	A = A >> 2	2
&=	A &= 2	A = A & 2	2
^=	A ^= 2	A = A ^ 2	8
|=	A |= 2	A = A | 2	10

Let's apply everything we have learned in this chapter by creating a Fibonacci program for up to 12 numbers.

```cpp
#include<iostream>

using namespace std;

main()
{
   int a, b, n1 = 0, n2 = 1, next;

   cout << "Enter the number of terms of Fibonacci series you want" << endl;
```

```cpp
    cin >> a;

    cout << "First " << a << " terms of Fibonacci series are :- " <<
endl;

    for ( b = 0 ; b < a ; b++ )
    {
      if ( b <= 1 )
        next = b;
      else
      {
        next = n1 + n2;
        n1 = n2;
        n2 = next;
      }
      cout << next << endl;
    }

    return 0;
}
```

Depending on your input, the result will differ. Run the program and discover what the output will look like.

C++ Capabilities

Considering the uniqueness of the C++ programming language, it has the following capabilities

- An object-oriented language supports aggregation, multiple inheritance, and dynamic behavior.
- It is highly portable
- It supports operator overload to work naturally with user-defined classes
- It gives developers a whole lot of choices in terms of design and coding.
- It doesn't require any graphic environment
- It is compatible with C

C++ Limitations

- It is difficult to debug when used for complex web application
- It does have security
- Normally used for specific platform application
- It doesn't support garbage collection
- Doesn't support built-in threads
- It is not secure because it has friend function, pointer, global variable

Chapter Five: SQL

Introduction

Structured Query Language (SQL) is a standard language designed for a relational database management system to help manage data effectively. It is a programming language precisely designed for the storage, retrieval, managing, and manipulation of data relational database management system (RDBMS).

It is hard to perform any database activity without using SQL because it is supported by various prominent relational database systems such as Oracle, SQL Server, and MySQL. Furthermore, some features available in the standard SQL are implemented differently in various database systems.

IBM developed this query language originally in the early 1970s. Originally, it wasn't called SQL but SEQUEL (Structured English Query Language) before it was changed to SQL. You are in for a wonderful adventure because this aspect of this book will help you learn and understand the basics of SQL.

Pre-requisites for Learning SQL

Since this book is for beginners, I am assuming that you don't have any knowledge about the database. My goal is to help you understand the basic concepts of SQL Languages. however, SQL is a declarative query language used for creating and manipulating databases. It doesn't require rocket science to understand the basic concepts because its syntax is simple and easy to understand when compared to other programming languages.

Nevertheless, foundational knowledge of relational database management system and a keen interest to study the language is my own prerequisites you need to start your journey of learning SQL.

What can you do with SQL?

You can use SQL for a whole lot of things, which includes:

- Create a database
- Create tables in a database
- Request or query information from a database
- Insert records
- Update or modify records in a database
- Delete records from a database
- Establish permissions or full control access in the database

The list below is just the tip of the iceberg of what you can do with SQL.

Topics to Cover in SQL

This chapter covers all fundamental concepts of SQL language like creating database and table, adding records to tables, using constraints, selecting records from tables, updating and deleting records in a table. The list is endless.

Once you have familiarized yourself with the basics, you will learn the methods of retrieving records by searching records, joining multiple tables, etc. In the end, I will highlight some advance concept in SQL such as performing aggregations and modifying an existing table structure.

What is SQL?

SQL is a computer language used for storing, manipulating, and retrieving of data stored in a relational database management system. A query language as stated earlier is used for accessing and modifying data in a database.

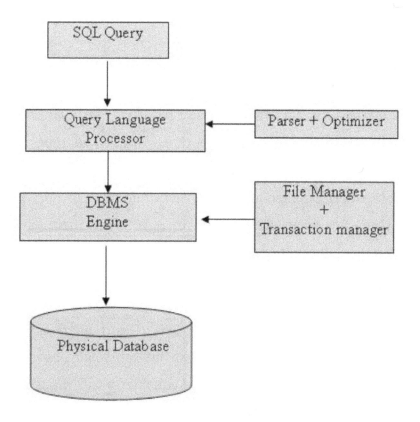

Before you can begin experimenting with SQL, you must have access to a database system. There are various online SQL editors you can use to evaluate or test SQL statements I have provided as examples in this book. However, you need a full-fledged database management system in order to execute SQL statements.

Basic Terms

What is Relational Database?

A relational database is a type of database categorized into tables with each table relating to another within the database. It allows data to be divided into smaller, logical, and manageable units for better performance and easier maintenance. To relate one table to another, you need to create a common field or key in a relational database system.

Definition Data

Data is a fact that relates to a particular object under consideration. For instance, your name, weight, height, weights are unique to you. You can also consider a file, image, or picture as data.

Definition Database

A database is a systematical collection of data. Through a database, you can manipulate and manage data easily. For instance, your electricity supply has a database to manage your billing, address, and other relevant information. Another example is your famous Facebook account; it contains information relating to your friends, messages, member activities, pictures, etc.

Definition Database Management System

DBMS is a collection of programs enables users to access database, report, manipulate, and represent data. Furthermore, it allows users to control access to the database. DBMS is not a new concept and was first implemented in the 1960s.

Types of Database Management System

- **Hierarchical DBMS** – this uses a "parent-child" relationship in storing data. People hardly use them nowadays. However, it has the structure of a tree with nodes representing records. An example of this type of DBMS is the registry used in Windows XP

- **Network DBMS** – This DBMS allows many-to-many relationship. For beginners, this is a complicated database structure. An example is the RDM server.

- **Relational DBMS** – This kind of DBMS defines a database relationship in terms of tables. Unlike the network DBMS, relational DBMS doesn't allow many-to-many relationship. Example of relational DBMS includes a Microsoft SQL Server database, Oracle, and MySQL.

- **Object-Oriented Relation DBMS** – This allows the storage of new data types. Data are stored in the form of objects

Setting Your SQL Work Environment

Peradventure you don't have any database management system in your computer, you can opt for various free open source database management system. You can decide to opt for the famous MySQL, which can be downloaded for both Windows and Linux operating systems.

Furthermore, you can install SQL Server Express, which is a free version of Microsoft SQL Server. Otherwise, you can decide to install XAMPP or WampServer. The WampServer is a Windows web development environment that allows you to create a MySQL database, PHP, and Apache2.

SQL Syntax

SQL Statements – These statements are simple and straightforward like your normal English language. However, they have specific syntax. Don't form your own meaning when you see some of the common English words you are conversant within this chapter.

An SQL statement comprises of a series of keywords, identifiers, etc. and ends with a semicolon (;). The following is an example of a SQL statement:

```
SELECT stu_name, DoB, age FROM studentFile Where age > 20;
```

The statement may look clumsy but for better readability, you can rewrite it in this format.

SELECT stu_name, DoB, age
FROM StudentFile
WHERE age > 20;

The purpose of the semicolon is to submit the statement to the database server or terminates the SQL statement.

Case Sensitivity in SQL

Keywords in SQL are not case sensitive like the previous languages discussed in this book. For instance, the keyword SELECT is the same as the select. However, depending on the operating system, the table names and database can be case-sensitive. Generally, Linux and UNIX platforms are case-sensitive, unlike Windows platforms that are not case-sensitive.

The example below retrieves records from the studentFile table

SELECT stu_name, DoB, age FROM studentFile;
select stu_name, DoB, age from studentFile;

The first one capitalizes the keywords whereas the second isn't capitalized. It is better to write SQL keywords in uppercase in order to differentiate it from other text.

SQL Comments

Similar to other programming languages, SQL comments are ignored and provide quick explanations concerning the SQL statements. You can either use a single-line or multi-line comments when writing comments in SQL. The two examples below will distinguish both comment writing formats.

```
--Select all the students
SELECT *FROM studentFile;
```

To write a multi-line comment, you use the /* with the statements followed by the */.

```
/* Select all the students
 whose age is greater than 20*/
SELECT *FROM studentFile
WHERE age > 20;
```

Database Creation

Before you can work with data, the first thing to do is to create a database. I am assuming you have installed the SQL Server or have MySQL in your system. Furthermore, ensure to allow every necessary privilege needed.

There are two ways of creating a database

- Using the simple SQL query
- Using MySQL

Simple SQL Query

The syntax for creating a database in SQL is

CREATE DATABASE databaseName;

For the examples illustrated earlier, to create the table, we have to use:

CREATE DATABASE studentFile;

Note: You can also use CREATE SCHEMA rather than using CREATE DATABASE to create a database. Additionally, creating a database doesn't make it available for use. To select the database, you have to select the database using the USE statement. For instance, the USE studentFile; command will set the StudentFile database as the target database.

MySQL Database Creation

I will use a command line tool to create a database in MySQL.

Step 1: Invoking the MySQL command-line tool

To do this, you have to log into your MySQL server. You have to log in as a root user and enter your password when asked. If everything goes right, you will be able to issue SQL statements.

Step 2: Creating the database

To create the database "studentFile", you have to execute the following command.

mysql> CREATE DATABASE studentFile;

If the database was successful, you will see – Query OK, 1 row affected (0.03 sec). However, if the database already exists, an error message will display. Therefore, to avoid such situation, you can include an optional clause – IF NOT EXISTS. To apply it to the example, it will be written as:

mysql> CREATE DATABASE IF NOT EXISTS studentFile;

Step 3: Selecting the Database

If the database already exists and you use the IF NOT EXISTS statement, to select this new database as the default database, you have to select it.

mysql > USE studentFile;

Tip – in order to see all the list of existing databases when using MySQL server, you can use the "SHOW DATABASES" keyword to execute it.

Creating Tables in SQL

So far, I am convinced you now know how to create a database. It is time to upgrade your knowledge in SQL by creating a table inside our database. The table will hold the data in the database. The purpose of the table is to organize your data or information into columns and rows.

The syntax for table creation

CREATE TABLE tableName (

    Column1_name data_type constraints,
    Column2_name data_type constraints,
    Column3_name data_type constraints,
);

For better understanding, I will create a table in our studentFile database using the MySQL command-line tool. The code below simplifies that.

```
-- Syntax for MySQL Database
CREATE TABLE studentRecord (
   id INT NOT NULL PRIMARY KEY AUTO_INCREMENT,
   Studname VARCHAR(50) NOT NULL,
   DoB DATE,
   phoneNum VARCHAR(15) NOT NULL UNIQUE

-- Syntax for SQL Server Database
CREATE TABLE studentRecord (
```

```
    id INT NOT NULL PRIMARY KEY IDENTITY(1,1),
    Studname VARCHAR(50) NOT NULL,
    DoB DATE,
    phoneNum VARCHAR(15) NOT NULL UNIQUE
);
```

The code above creates a table named studentRecord with five columns id, Studname, DoB, and phoneNum. If you observe, a data type declaration succeeds each column name.

In a database table, every column must have a name followed by a data type. The developer decides on the particular to use, depending on the information to store in each column. From the example above, some statement looks "foreign" and requires explanations. Later, I will talk about the various data types but to familiarize yourself with them, they include:

- Exact numcric
- Approximate numeric
- Date and time
- Character strings
- Unicode character strings
- Binary strings
- Other data types

Besides the data type, there are constraints used in the code. Constraints are rules defined concerning the values permitted in columns. The following constraints were mentioned.

- The PRIMARY KEY constrains, which marks the corresponding field as the primary key for the table
- The NOT NULL constraints, which make sure fields cannot accept an unacceptable value
- The AUTO_INCREMENT attribute, which automatically assigns a value to a field left unspecified. It increases the previous value by 1 and only available for numerical fields.
- The UNIQUE constraint ensures every single row contains a unique value in the table

In a similar fashion, you can use the IF NOT EXIST statement we used when creating a database to overwrite an existing table. This is important as it avoids any already existing table. Alternatively, if you want to display available tables, you can use the SHOW TABLES statement.

```
CREATE TABLE IF NOT EXISTS studentRecords (
    id INT NOT NULL PRIMARY KEY AUTO_INCREMENT,
    Studname VARCHAR(40) NOT NULL, DoB,
    phoneNum VARCHAR(25) NOT NULL UNIQUE
);
```

Constraints In SQL

As the name implies, it is a restriction or limitation imposed on a column (s) of a table in order to place a limitation on the type of values the table can store. They provide a better mechanism to retain the reliability and accuracy of the data contained in the table. We have several categories of constraints, which includes:

NOT NULL Constraint – This statement states that NULL values will not be accepted at the column. What it means is that a new row cannot be added in a table without the inclusion of a non-NULL value for such a column.

For instance, the statement below creates a table "studentRecords" with four columns and three of these columns (id, Studname, and phoneNum) do not accept NULL Values.

```
CREATE TABLE studentRecords (
  id INT NOT NULL,
  Studname VARCHAR(30) NOT NULL,
  DoB DATE,
  phoneNum VARCHAR(15) NOT NULL
);
```

Tip: A null value is not the same as blank, zero (0), or a zero-length character string. The meaning of a NULL is that there hasn't been any entry made in that field.

- **PRIMARY KEY Constraint** – This classifies a column (s) with values that distinctively recognize a row in the table. You cannot have two rows simultaneously in a particular table having the same value for its primary key. The example below shows a SQL statement creating a table named "studentRecords" and identify the id column as the primary key.

```
CREATE TABLE studentRecords (
  id INT NOT NULL PRIMARY KEY,
  Studname VARCHAR(30) NOT NULL,
  DoB DATE,
  phoneNum VARCHAR(15) NOT NULL
);
```

- **UNIQUE Constraint** – if you want to restrict a column (s) to contain unique values in a table, the UNIQUE statement is used. While the PRIMARY KEY and UNIQUE constraint enforce uniqueness in a table; however, the UNIQUE constraint is used when your goal is to enforce the exclusivity on a particular column (s). I will use our previous example to specify the phone column as unique. With this, the phone column won't allow duplicated values.

```
CREATE TABLE studentRecords (
  id INT NOT NULL PRIMARY KEY,
  Studname VARCHAR(30) NOT NULL,
  DoB DATE,
  phoneNum VARCHAR(15) NOT NULL UNIQUE,
  country VARCHAR(30) NOT NULL DEFAULT 'England'
);
```

- **FOREIGN KEY Constraint** – This particular kind of constraint is a column (s) used to set up and implement a relationship among data in two different tables.
- **CHECK constraint** – The purpose of this statement is to restrict values in a column. For instance, the range of student age column can be restricted by creating CHECK constraint, which allows values only 16 to 45. This hinders ages entered from exceeding the age range. Here is an example to illustrate it.

```
CREATE TABLE studentRecords (
    stu_id INT NOT NULL PRIMARY KEY,
    stu_name VARCHAR(55) NOT NULL,
    stu_date DATE NOT NULL,
    age INT NOT NULL CHECK (age >= 16 AND age <= 45),
    dept_id INT,
    FOREIGN KEY (dept_id) REFERENCES
departments(dept_id)
);
```

Inserting Data in Tables

In previous examples, I created a table with the name "studentRecords" in our "studentFile" database. Now, we need to add information into the table. To do this, SQL has a unique keyword, which is the "INSERT INTO" statement.

Format:

INSERT INTO NameOfTable (columnA, columnB, columnC,...)
VALUES (value1, value2, value3,...);

The syntax is self-explanatory but if you are unclear, the tableName is the name of your table. In our examples so far, we have used "studentRecords." However, the column1, column2, column3,... represents the name of the table columns with value1, value2, value3 the parallel values for the columns.

To insert records to our "studentRecords" table, we will use the following statement.

INSERT INTO studentRecords (FullName, Age, Sex, PhoneNum) ;
VALUES ('Donald Williamson', '30', 'Male', '0722-022569') ;

If you observe, there is no value inserted for the id field. Do you remember when we created the table (studentRecords), we mark the id field with an AUTO_INCREMENT flag. Let's add another record to our table.

INSERT INTO studentRecords (FullName, Age, Sex, PhoneNum) ;
VALUES ('Jefferson Peterson', '45', 'Male', '0252-027948') ;

Why don't you add another one?

INSERT INTO studentRecords (FullName, Age, Sex, PhoneNum) ;
VALUES ('Mariah Lawson', '50', 'Female', '0722-457906') ;

If you were to display the output of this table, it will look like this

133

id	FullName	Age	Sex	PhoneNum
1	Donald Williamson	30	Male	0722-022569
2	Jefferson Peterson	45	Male	0252-027948
3	Mariah Lawson	50	Female	0722-457906

So far, I am convinced without any doubt that creating a database shouldn't be an issue. The same applies to create a table and inserting records. However, what if you want to retrieve the content of a table, how will you go about that? The next section will clarify that.

Selecting Data in a Table

If you want to retrieve data in a table, the "SELECT" statement is what you will use. This statement can retrieve all information in the rows in one time as long as it satisfies the condition stated.

Format

SELECT column1_name, column2_name, FROM tableName;

Note: This system is for specific columns. However, if your goal is to select the entire, consider the syntax below:

SELECT *FROM tableName;

Note: Whenever you see an asterisk (*) in SQL, just know it is a wildcard character, which signifies everything. It copies all the content.

Let's use the information we inserted when we used the "INSERT INTO" statement.

id	FullName	Age	Sex	PhoneNum
1	Donald Williamson	30	Male	0722-022569
2	Jefferson Peterson	45	Male	0252-027948
3	Mariah Lawson	50	Female	0722-457906

If we use the "SELECT *FROM studentRecords;" it will display the following information.

id	FullName	Age	Sex	PhoneNum
1	Donald Williamson	30	Male	0722-022569
2	Jefferson Peterson	45	Male	0252-027948
3	Mariah Lawson	50	Female	0722-457906

Perhaps, you only need certain information in the table, you use specific columns. Assuming we want to select only the id, FullName, and sex. It will look like this.

```
SELECT id, FullName, Sex
FROM studentRecords;
```

After executing this statement, the output will be

id	FullName	Sex
1	Donald Williamson	Male
2	Jefferson Peterson	Male
3	Mariah Lawson	Female

SQL WHERE Statement

By now, I know you can fetch records in a table column or all the records in the table. However, in a real-world situation, we need to delete, update, or select records that fulfill certain criteria such as those in a particular age, country, or group. In this section, I will expound how we can use the "WHERE" clause.

Syntax

SELECT columnList FROM tableName WHERE condition;

The columList include fields/column like name, country, age, phone, etc. of a table. Furthermore, if you want all the values of the various columns, you can use the syntax below.

SELECT * FROM tableName WHERE condition

Let me use an example to explain the SELECT statement assuming the table name is "studentRecords."

id	FullName	Age	Sex	PhoneNum
1	Donald Williamson	30	Male	0722-022569
2	Jefferson Peterson	45	Male	0252-027948
3	Mariah Lawson	50	Female	0722-457906
4	Jackson Fred	32	Male	0721-487924
5	Venus Sean	38	Female	0787-972853
6	Merkel Hassan	36	Female	0978-216597

Filtering records using WHERE clause

Using the table above, I want to return all students whose age is above 30. We can use the WHERE clause to remove unwanted data.

```
SELECT *FROM studentRecords WHERE age >35;
```

After executing this statement, the output will look like this:

id	FullName	Age	Sex	PhoneNum
2	Jefferson Peterson	45	Male	0252-027948
3	Mariah Lawson	50	Female	0722-457906
5	Venus Sean	38	Female	0787-972853
6	Merkel Hassan	36	Female	0978-216597

The statement below will fetch all the record of the student with id 4

```
SELECT *FROM studentRecords WHERE id = 4;
```
The output will be:

id	FullName	Age	Sex	PhoneNum
4	Jackson Fred	32	Male	0721-487924

You can combine certain operates with the "WHERE" clause. The table below summarizes the important operators used in SQL.

Operator	Description	Example
=	Equal	WHERE id = 4
>	Greater than	WHERE age > 30
<	Less than	WHERE age < 25
<=	Less than or equivalent to	WHERE price <= 900
>=	Greater than or equivalent to	WHERE age >= 15
LIKE	Simple pattern matching	WHERE name LIKE 'Dav'
IN	Check whether a specified value matches any value in a list or subquery	WHERE Country IN ('BRAZIL', 'SWEDEN')
BETWEEN	Check whether a specified value is within a range of values	WHERE age BETWEEN 3 AND 5

The AND operator

The SQL language gives developers the opportunity to use the AND and OR operators to fetch specific records from a table. The AND operator is used to combine two conditions while returning true only when both conditions are true.

Format:

SELECT columnName1, columnName2 FROM tableName WHERE condition1 AND condition2;

The example below will demonstrate how the AND operator works.

id	FullName	Age	Sex	PhoneNum	Dept_No
1	Donald Williamson	30	Male	0722-022569	0101

2	Jefferson Peterson	45	Male	0252-027948	0102
3	Mariah Lawson	50	Female	0722-457906	0103
4	Jackson Fred	32	Male	0721-487924	0104
5	Venus Sean	38	Female	0787-972853	0105
6	Merkel Hassan	36	Female	0978-216597	NULL

```
SELECT *FROM studentRecords
WHERE age > 30 AND Dept_No = 0104;
```

After execution, the output will look like this:

id	FullName	Age	Sex	PhoneNum	Dept_No
4	Jackson Fred	32	Male	0721-487924	0104

The OR Operator

This operator combines two different conditions; however, if one or both conditions are true, it returns true. Assuming you want the record of students whose age is greater than 40 or the Dept_No is equal to 0104.

```
SELECT *FROM studentRecords
WHERE age > 40 OR Dept_No = 0104;
```

The output will be:

id	FullName	Age	Sex	PhoneNum	Dept_No
2	Jefferson Peterson	45	Male	0252-027948	0102
3	Mariah Lawson	50	Female	0722-457906	0103
4	Jackson Fred	32	Male	0721-487924	0104

Furthermore, you can combine the "AND" and "OR" operator to create compound expressions. Consider the statement below.

```
SELECT *FROM studentRecords
WHERE age > 40 AND (Dept_No = 102 or Dept_No=103);
```

After execution, the output will be:

id	FullName	Age	Sex	PhoneNum	Dept_No
2	Jefferson Peterson	45	Male	0252-027948	0102
3	Mariah Lawson	50	Female	0722-457906	0103

SQL UPDATE STATEMENT

You have learned how to insert data including selecting a particular data from a table under certain condition (s). However, over time students or employee information may require updating such as location, phone number, address, etc. SQL has a unique statement that allows you to update your table without having to create a new table.

Format:

```
UPDATE tableName
SET column1Name = value1, column2Name = value2,...
colunmNamen = valueN
WHERE condition;
```

In the syntax above, column1_name, column2_name are the names of the fields or columns of a table whose value you want to update. You can also use the combination of the "AND" and "OR" operator to update statements in the table. Let me use an example to demonstrate the update statement.

id	FullName	Age	Sex	PhoneNum	Dept_No
1	Donald Williamson	30	Male	0722-022569	0101
2	Jefferson Peterson	45	Male	0252-027948	0102
3	Mariah Lawson	50	Female	0722-457906	0103
4	Jackson Fred	32	Male	0721-487924	0104
5	Venus Sean	38	Female	0787-972853	0105
6	Merkel Hassan	36	Female	0978-216597	NULL

To update the student record of Venus Sean to Venus Williams Sean, the statement will be

```
UPDATE studentRecords SET FullName = "Venus Williams
Sean"
WHERE id =5;
```

The output will be:

id	FullName	Age	Sex	PhoneNum	Dept_No
1	Donald Williamson	30	Male	0722-022569	0101
2	Jefferson Peterson	45	Male	0252-027948	0102
3	Mariah Lawson	50	Female	0722-457906	0103
4	Jackson Fred	32	Male	0721-487924	0104
5	Venus Williams Sean	38	Female	0787-972853	0105
6	Merkel Hassan	36	Female	0978-216597	NULL

SQL DELETE

Finally, you have learned how to insert, select, and update information in a table. However, it is important to know how to delete a specific field or entire table especially if the table has fulfilled its purpose.

Format:

DELETE FROM table_name WHERE condition;

Using the table below, let us delete some records from the student's record created.

id	FullName	Age	Sex	PhoneNum	Dept_No
1	Donald Williamson	30	Male	0722-022569	0101
2	Jefferson Peterson	45	Male	0252-027948	0102
3	Mariah Lawson	50	Female	0722-457906	0103
4	Jackson Fred	32	Male	0721-487924	0104
5	Venus Sean	38	Female	0787-972853	0105
6	Merkel Hassan	36	Female	0978-216597	NULL

DELETE FROM studentRecords WHERE id >4;

After execution, the outcome will be as follow:

id	FullName	Age	Sex	PhoneNum	Dept_No
1	Donald Williamson	30	Male	0722-022569	0101

2	Jefferson Peterson	45	Male	0252-027948	0102
3	Mariah Lawson	50	Female	0722-457906	0103
4	Jackson Fred	32	Male	0721-487924	0104

However, to delete the entire data in a table, there isn't any need to use the WHERE clause. To delete all records in the "studentRecords" table, you have to use the statement below.

```
DELETE FROM studentRecords;
```

Chapter Six: Introduction to Java Programming

Welcome to your fifth programming course in this book. Indeed, you have progressed beyond your expectation. Did you think you could do it at the beginner? Nobody is born a programmer rather by learning and putting it to practice, they become good at it.

Welcome to Java Programming. I will introduce you to Java in its simplicity. Java is one of the most interesting and practicable programs to learn as a beginner. At the end of this chapter, you will become a professional computer programmer.

As I always tell beginners, programming is easy. At first, many consider Java as a hard language to understand but after familiarizing themselves with the environment, they discover it is quite easy to learn. It doesn't matter your programming experience or level, this chapter was written putting various things into consideration. As you expand your programming knowledge, you will discover that you will be a top-notch programmer in all areas.

In spite of the numerous programming languages in the world, Java is one of the languages in high demand. If you dedicate your time into studying the environment, you are literally setting yourself into a fast-growing career in the next few years. Java programming skills are sought after because of its flexibility, readability, and simplicity. Presently, if you are a Java programmer or developer in the United States of American, you will be earning nothing less than $85k annual salary. Do you still think Java programming is worth learning?

Pre-requisite for Learning Java

You must know the basics of how to use a computer system. However, if you are a beginner to programming, then you need to understand the fundamental to programming. If you already know programming languages like C, C++ or any object-oriented language, then Java should be an easy language for you to learn.

Concepts of Java Programming

Since the demands for breaking through various hurdles of coding extremely large projects, we have seen the advent of object-oriented programming. This has led to the combination of some of the best methodologies of structured programming along with new concepts. In this section, I want to briefly explain some of these programming concepts in Java Programming.

Encapsulation

From the name, you can have an idea of what encapsulation entails. Encapsulation in a layman term is a method that binds the programming code along with data it operates while keeping them safe from exterior interference. An object is formed when these data and code are connected with each other. This object can be private or public; if it is private, the data or code will be inaccessible by any program that exists out the object. However, if it is public, it can be accessible by other programs even if they are not within the object.

Polymorphism

Another important concept of Java Programming is polymorphism, which involves creating a particular interface for several methods. The significance is that it reduces program complication by permitting the same interface.

Inheritance

This concept involves an object receiving the same features or properties of another object that supports it. For instance, you have a watermelon, which is of the classification of watermelon. It also belongs to a fruit class that is part of a larger class known as food. This food class has features that make it nutritious and edible. Additionally, the fruits can be sweet and juicy. Therefore, combining these features and other things makes up the watermelon.

Understanding the Java Environment

It is important to understand the Java environment and I will start by telling you how you can install the software on your computer. After installation, you can start with the basic "Hello World" program.

Before starting up, you need to be sure that your computer has what it takes to write Java programs. It is advisable to check websites that offer the language free. You can visitwww.oracle.com/technetwork/java/javase/downloadsor www.java.com to install the software on your system.

Basically, what you will need to write Java programs include

- JDK (Java Development Kit)
- Text Editor (NotePad, TextPad, Atom, Sublime for windows; for Mac – gEdit, jEdit, Atom while for Ubuntu, you can use gEdit)

The language is a high-level programming language, which means you cannot run it on your computer directly. For you to run the program on your system it needs to be translated to the language the computer understands and this is where the javac compiler comes to play. The compiler takes the java code and translates it to machine code.

Java Virtual Machine is a virtual machine that resides on your computer. Its role is to make it easier for the compiler to generate byte code for the machine. JVM is a program that makes it easier to run a java platform independently.

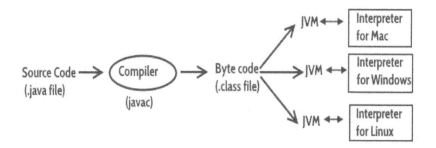

Running Your First Java Program

Tighten your seat belt because here is where the real thing starts. In this aspect, I will show you the easiest way to write java programs, compile them, and finally execute them. let's start with the simple program.

```
public class BeginnersProgram {
  public static void main(String[] args){
    System.out.println("Hello World, This is my first programming practice in java.");
  }//End of main
}//End of FirstJavaProgram Class
```

Output

```
Hello World, This is my first programming practice in java.
```

Explanation

public class MyFirstJaveProgram {

this is the beginning of a java program. All java application must have at least a class definition, which comprises of the class keyword accompanied by the class name. From the first line, you can see that the class is public

public static void main(String[] args){

This statement makes the main method to be "public". What it means is that you can call the method from outside the class. The void in the statement signifies that it doesn't return anything whereas *main* is a method name. It is the starting point where the program begins execution. Additionally, the (String[] args) is a command line argument

System.out.printlin ("Hello World, This is my first programming practice in java.")

This statement prints out the content of what is in the quotes to the console while inserting a newline.

Variables

I believe you know what a variable is as you have gone through various programming languages in this book. The variable is allocated a value during the program. Its value changes in the course of the program. For instance, int number1 = 12;

In this example, number1 is a variable name where 12 is the value assigned to it. On the other hand, int is a data type that declares "number1" as a variable.

Declaring Variables in Java

Syntax:

data_type variableName = value;

It is compulsory in Java to have the data type and variable name but the value is optional you can allocate value to a variable after declaring it. For instance, in the previous example, I declared number1 as a variable with data type as an integer. In the next section, I will talk more about data types.

Convention in Variable naming in Java

- Variable names are case sensitive
- Variable names can start with special characters such as underscore and dollar sign ($)
- Variable names cannot contain whitespace. For instance, int student = 40; this is not valid because of the space the variable contains
- Variable names must start with a small letter. For instance number1; however, if the variable is lengthy, you can use capital little like this – numberStudent1, NewBus, etc.

Types of Variables

Variables are of three types in Java.

Local Variable

You declare these variables inside the method of a class. Furthermore, the scopes of these variables are limited to the method. Their values cannot be changed and accessed outside the method. From the example below, the instance variable is declared having the same local variable name. The essence of this is to show the scope of the local variable scope. Study the program properly because missing any step here will affect you later.

```
public class VariableExa {
    // I want to declare the instance variable at this point
    public String myVar="instance variable";
// declaration of instance variable done
    public void myMethod(){
        // Here I am declaring our local variable
        String myVar = "Inside Method";
        System.out.println(myVar);
    }
    public static void main(String args[]){
        // This area creates the object
        VariableExa obj = new VariableExa();
```

```
    /* we call the variable name, which changes myVar value.
     * Furthermore, myVar will be displayed after
     * the method call, to indicate that the
     * scope of the local variable is restricted to only the method.
     */
    System.out.println("Calling Method");
    obj.myMethod();
    System.out.println(obj.myVar);
  }
}
```

The output of this program after execution will be:

```
Calling Method
Inside Method
instance variable
```

Static Variable

Some programmers refer to it as a class variable because of its association with the class. For instance, if you create four different objects; however, these objects have the same class with access to the static variable, the static variable will be common for all object. In order words, an alteration to the variable through the use of a single object will literally imitate others when accessed through the other objects. Consider the program below that illustrates the use of a static variable.

```java
public class StaticExa {
  public static String ClassVar="class or static variable";

  public static void main(String args[]){
    StaticExa obj = new StaticExa();
    StaticExa objA = new StaticExa();
    StaticExa objB = new StaticExa();

    //The three objects will display "class or static variable"
    System.out.println(obj.ClassVar);
    System.out.println(objA.ClassVar);
    System.out.println(objB.ClassVar);

    //altering the static variable value through objA
    objA.ClassVar = "Text Changed";

    //The three objects will display "Text Changed for object"
    System.out.println(obj.ClassVar);
    System.out.println(objA.ClassVar);
    System.out.println(objB.ClassVar);
  }
}
```

The output of the program will be:

```
class or static variable
class or static variable
class or static variable
Text Changed for object
Text Changed for object
Text Changed object
```

Instance Variable

This variable is the opposite of the static variable because every single object within a class contains its own duplicate, unlike the static variable that contains the same object. From the example below, the value of the instance variable (obj2) is changed and when displayed with other objects, others remained unchanged, unlike the obj2.

```java
public class InstanceExa {
  String InstanceVar="My Instance variable";

  public static void main(String args[]){
      InstanceExa obj = new InstanceExa();
      InstanceExa objA = new InstanceExa();
      InstanceExa objB = new InstanceExa();

      System.out.println(obj.InstanceVar);
```

```
        System.out.println(objA.InstanceVar);
        System.out.println(objB.InstanceVar);


        objA.InstanceVar = "Text Changed for Variable";


        System.out.println(obj.InstanceVar);
        System.out.println(objA.InstanceVar);
        System.out.println(objB.InstanceVar);
    }
}
```

The output of the program will be:

```
My Instance variable
My Instance variable
My Instance variable
My Instance variable
Text Changed for Variable
My Instance variable
```

Now, observe the difference between the static variable and the instance variable. Did you notice any major difference? Let us move into something more important – data types.

Data Types

The meaning of data type is the same whether it is Java, C, C++, or SQL. The data type defines that particular value a variable can accommodate. For instance, a variable of integer data type has the capacity of only accommodating integer values. Nevertheless, data types are of two types in Java. These are primitive and non-primitive. Notwithstanding, my focus in this book is on the primitive data types. For clarity purpose, you should know that non-Primitive data types include strings and arrays.

Java Programming Primitive Data Types

Generally, Java has eight primitive data types and these include int, short, Boolean, char, long, byte, double and float. These data types are the same irrespective of the operating system you are using.

Int

This data type is used to hold integer variables and ranges from -2,147,483,648 up until 2,147,483,647. It has a default size and value of 4 bytes and 0 respectively. The example below shows the variable "number1" declared as an integer data type and printed out.

159

```
class DataTypeExample {
   public static void main(String[] args) {
// Declaration of variables
        number1 = 1250;
        System.out.println(number1);
   }
}
```

Outcome:

```
1250
```

Byte

A byte data type can only hold numbers between 128 and 127. It has a data size and value of 1 byte and 0 respectively. Study the program below.

```
class DataTypeExample {
   public static void main(String[] args) {
   // declaration of NewNum as byte
        byte NewNum;

        NewNum = 80;
        System.out.println(NewNum);
```

```
        }
}
```

Output:

```
80
```

Now, let us consider another example of the byte data type.

```
class DataTypeExample {
    public static void main(String[] args) {

        byte NewNumber;

        NewNumber = 180;
        System.out.println(NewNumber);
    }
}
```

What will be the result now? If your answer is 180, you are obviously wrong. Are you surprised? Do you remember the byte data type range is between -128 and 127? Therefore, if you execute the above program, you will get a type mismatch error because 180 is beyond the range data type.

Short

In terms of size, it is greater than the byte data and has a default size of 2 bytes. It has a data range of 32,768 to 32767.

```
class DataTypeExample {
  public static void main(String[] args) {
      // Declaration of the variable
      short number1;

      number1 = 18000;
      System.out.println(number1);
  }
}
```

The output will be:

18000

Long

You can use this data type when the int data type isn't big enough to accommodate the value you want to use. It ranges from -9,223,372,036,854,775,808 to 9,223,372,036,854,775,807 and has a size of 8 bytes.

```
class DataTypeExample {
  public static void main(String[] args) {
// declaration of the variable to demonstrate long data type
      long number1= -48972698741L;
```

```
        System.out.println(number1);
    }
}
```

Output

-48972698741

Double

This holds up to 15 decimal numbers and has a size of 8 bytes.

```
class DataTypeExample {
    public static void main(String[] args) {
//declaration of variable

        double number1 = -789874437.9d

        System.out.println(number1);
    }
}
```

What will be the Output:

-4.145898371E7

Char

This holds characters and has a size of 2 bytes.

```
class DataTypeExample {
```

```
public static void main(String[] args) {
    // declaration of variable Myname as char
    char Myname = 'Johnson';

    System.out.println(Myname);
  }
}
```

Output

Johnson

Boolean

This either holds true or false value.

```
class DataTypeExample {
  public static void main(String[] args) {
// performing Boolean operation using true and false

        Boolean light = True;

        System.out.println(light);
  }
}
```

The Output will be:

True

Float

This holds 6 to 7 decimal number and has a size of 4 bytes.

```
class DataTypeExample {
    public static void main(String[] args) {
float number1 = 20.70f;
        System.out.println(number1);
    }
}
```

Output

20.70

<u>Summary of primitive data types</u>

- If you want to store whole numbers, you can use long, short, byte, and int data types
- char is used for storing letters
- double and float for fractional numbers
- Boolean for variables that hold true or false

Operators in Java Programming

This section describes available operators you can use in the course of your coding. You can use them to manipulate variables or create complex programs. Normally, you can use these operators to compare, modify, and control data within the Java environment. The basic operators in Java include:

Arithmetic Operators

You are already familiar with these operators and they include addition (+), subtraction (-), multiplication (*), division (/), and modulo (%). I will use a simple program to illustrate these operators.

```
public class ArithmeticOperator {
  public static void main(String args[]) {
// declaration of profit and loss as integer to perform the
arithmetic operation
    int profit = 250;
    int loss = 70;

    System.out.println("profit + loss: " + (profit + loss) );
    System.out.println("profit – loss: " + (profit–loss) );
    System.out.println("profit * loss: " + (profit * loss) );
    System.out.println("profit/ loss: " + (profit / loss) );
    System.out.println("profit % loss: " + (profit % loss) );
  }
}
```

The Output of this program will be:

```
profit + loss: 320
profit– loss: 180
profit * loss: 22400
```

profit / loss: 3.5714
profit % loss: 60

Assignment Operator

These operators include =, +=, -=, *=, /=, and %=

Income=expenses this assigns the value of the variable expenses to Income

Income +=expenses is equivalent to Income = Income + expenses

Income -=expenses is equivalent to Income = Income − expenses

Income*=expenses is equivalent to Income = Income * expenses

Income/=expenses is equivalent to Income = Income/expenses

Income%=expenses is equivalent to Income = Income % expenses

Consider the program above to illustrate the use of assignment operators

```
public class AssignOpe {
  public static void main(String args[]) {
    int income = 10;
    int expenses = 20;
```

```java
expenses += income ;
    System.out.println("+= Output: "+expenses);


expenses = income ;
    System.out.println("= Output: "+expenses);


    expenses -= income ;
    System.out.println("-= Output: "+expenses);

expenses /= income ;
    System.out.println("/= Output: "+expenses);


    expenses *= income ;
    System.out.println("*= Output: "+expenses);




    expenses %= income ;
    System.out.println("%= Output: "+expenses);
 }
}
```

The output of the program will be:

+= Output: 20	
= Output: 10	
-= Output: 10	
/= Output: 10	
*= Output: 100	
%= Output: 0	

Logical operator

These are used for conditional statements and loops to evaluate a condition. These operators are &&, !, and ||.

Operator	Meaning	Example
!	Logical Not. This evaluate true only if the operand is 0	If a=5 then, the expression! holds true.
&&	Logical AND. It returns true only when all the	If a =4 and b = 2; the expression ((a==4) && (a<4)) equals to

		operands are true.	0.
||		Logical OR. This evaluates to true when one operand returns true	If a =4 and b = 2; the expression ((a==4) && (a<4)) equals to 1.

Consider the program above.

```
public class LogicalOperator {
  public static void main(String args[]) {
// Declaration of variables
boolean No = false;
boolean Yes = true;


   System.out.println("Yes && No: " + (Yes&&No));

   System.out.println("!(Yes && No): " + !(Yes&&No));
   System.out.println("Yes || No: " + (Yes||No));
}


}
```

Output will be:

```
Yes && No: false
!(Yes && No): true
Yes || No: true
```

Conclusion

There are other operators available in Java; however, with the aforementioned operators, you can start programming. Finally, you have gotten to the end of the basics of Java programming. Don't stop here, put to practice everything you have learned and considered moving to advanced programming.

Chapter Seven: JavaScript Programming for Beginners

If there is anything I want you to hold at the end of this programming guide for JavaScript is the fact that:

- JavaScript is the HTML and web language
- It is easy to Learn

If you can do that, then at the end, you will smile your way to programming for the web. However, your speed in learning JavaScript and other programming language is very dependent on you. If you find yourself struggling, don't feel demoralized rather take a break and reread the material after you have settled down. Remember, this chapter gives you the basics of JavaScript as a beginner to familiarize yourself with the language.

Introduction

This JavaScript guide is written with the intention to help both beginners and professionals understand the programming language for the web more efficiently. JavaScript is a solution aimed at performing various actions dynamically. The JavaScript translator, which is rooted in the web browser such as Firefox, Google Chrome, Internet Explorer, Safari, etc., allows the interpretation of the JavaScript code.

JavaScript is an object-oriented scripting language, which is lightweight and works in cross-platform such as Mack, Linux, or Windows. If you want to create an interactive website for users, the place of JavaScript cannot be overemphasized.

What is JavaScript?

It is a scripting language created in 1995 by Netscape as a means of validating forms while offering interactive content for websites. The language has evolved over time with it being used by various web browsers.

Why should I Study JavaScript?

You should study JavaScript because it is among the three fundamental languages every web developer must learn and understand. With HTML, you can define your web page contents whereas CSS allows you to identify your web page layout; however, with JavaScript, you can program the actions of these web pages. You see the important role JavaScript plays in web pages.

Importance of JavaScript for Websites

- Displaying time and date
- Client-side validation of controls
- Displaying clocks

- Displaying popup windows and dialog boxes such as a prompt dialog box, confirmation dialog box, and an alert dialog box
- Display times such as online test
- Displaying animations

If you judiciously follow this guide, by the end, you will be a master of the art programming web pages.

Pre-requisites for learning JavaScript

Although, you will hear many developers educating beginners about the fact that there are no prerequisites to learning JavaScript. That is true because you can learn the language without having any programming foundation or knowledge. However, to expedite your learning process, you can improve yourself on basic courses such as:

- Discrete mathematics
- Algebra
- Algorithms in Data structures
- Learn a static language like C++ as it will give you the cutting-edge

Variables in JavaScript

Variables shouldn't be new if you went through Chapter two to Chapter six of this book. In a layman term, a variable is a memory location designed to store different values and assigned with a name. JavaScript uses the "var" keyword, accompanied by the variable name. For instance, to a name as a variable, you will use the statement below.

```
var exam = 50;
var test = 12;
var score = exam * test;
```

In the example above, exam, test, and score are variables given values with the value stored. We can perform various operations in JavaScript including multiplication, subtraction, addition, subtraction, and division. Variables and values can be declared as a number, string, or letter.

```
var name = "insert your name";
var number = '45';
```

From the example, you can enclose string with a single or double quote because they work exactly the same way.

JavaScript Identifiers

Every variable in JavaScript must have a unique name, which is used to identify it. These unique names are called identifiers. Identifiers have certain rules, which include:

- Every identifier must begin with a letter

- They can contain digits (0-9), letters (a-z), dollar signs ($), and underscores (_)
- Reserved words are not accepted
- Variable names are case sensitive
- An identifier can begin with a dollar sign or underscore.

Scope of JavaScript Variable

JavaScript allows two types of variable scope, which includes global and local variable scope. A variable is said to be global if it is declared outside the function body. With this, every statement has access to the variable within the same document. However, a local variable scope has its scope within the function. With this, the variable is only available to statements within the same function.

Data Types in JavaScript

Data types are important in JavaScript because it determines the type of value assigned to an identifier. Without data types, hardly can your computer solve any problem safely. JavaScript has two types of data types, which are:

Primitive data types

These are the primary blocks of any JavaScript program and includes:

- Numeric – You can use both floating numbers and integer in JavaScript. However, it doesn't support the use of decimal numbers.

- Strings – This is a group of characters encircled in either a single or a double quote. Every string must end with its corresponding quote – a single quote must always end with a single quote.

- Boolean – This involves logical values, whose value is either true or false. Boolean data type uses conditional statements.

- Null – this represents no value, which means strings are empty

The other data type used in JavaScript is the compositive data type. It is imperative to note that JavaScript data types are dynamic, that is, the same variable can be used to hold different data types. For instance,

```
var a;       // Now a is undefined
a = 89;       // Now a is a Number
a = "Germany";    // Now a is a String
```

The program below demonstrates the use of data type in JavaScript. The first one shows a JavaScript program that shows the summation of two floating numbers (test and exam) while the second one illustrates the use of Boolean data type.

```html
<html>
<head>
<script language="javascript">
function showAlert()
{
var test=22.50;
var exam=50.50;
var score=0;
score=test+exam;
document.write(" score= "+score);
document.write("\t\tHello\nworld!\n");
document.write('\nWelcome to JavaScript');
}
</script>
</head>
<body>

<script language="javascript">

showAlert();

</script>

</body>
</html>
```

The program below illustrates the use of Boolean expression. First, I allocate the value "0" to the variable "number." Then the user is prompted to enter a number, which must be within the range of 1 and 500. Nonetheless, If the user entered a number above the stated range (500), a message will be displayed on the screen indicating an error.. However, if the number falls within the 500 range, it will determine if the figured inputted is either equal or greater

```
<html>
<body>
<script type="text/javascript">
var number=0;
number=prompt("Enter a number");
document.write("Your entered number is :"+number);
if (number>=1 && number<10)
document.write("Your entered number is greater than 1 and less than 10");
else if(number>=10 && number<20)
document.write("Your entered number is greater than 10 and less than 20");
else if(number>=20 && number<30)
document.write("Your entered number is greater than 20 and less than 30");
else if(number>=30 && number<40)
document.write("Your entered number is greater than 30 and
```

```
less than 40");
else if(number>=40 && number<100)
document.write("Your entered number is greater than 40 and
less than 100");
else if(number>=100 && number<=500)
document.write("Your entered number is greater than 100 or less
than 500");
else
document.write("You did not enter any number!")
</script>
</body>
</html>
```

Operators in JavaScript

Operators are functions with arithmetic, bitwise or logical property. JavaScript also has its own operators to perform various operations. In this unit, I will explore the basic operators you can use as a beginner in JavaScript.

Arithmetic Operators

Operators	Meaning
+	Addition
-	Subtraction
/	Division

*	Multiplication
=	Assignment
%	Mod
--	Decrement
++	Increment

You should be conversant with some of these operators if you have gone through this book. However, I am not going to explain anything but illustrate each operator using a JavaScript program.

Addition

```
var number1 = 105;
var number2 = 25;
var total = number1+number2;          //total = 130
```

Subtraction

```
var number1 = 105;
var number2 = 25;
var total = number1-number2;          //total = 180
```

Multiplication

```
var number1 = 105;
var number2 = 25;
var total = number1*number2;          //total = 2625
```

Division

```
var number1 = 105;
var number2 = 25;
var total = number1/number2;          //total = 4.2
```

Mod

```
var number1 = 105;
var number2 = 25;
var total = number1%number2;          //total = 5
```

Assignment

```
var number1 = 105;
var number2 ;
number2 = number1;          //total = 105
```

Increment

```
var number1 = 105;
var number2 = number1++;     // number2 = 106
```

Decrement

```
var number1 = 105;
var number2 = number1--;     // number2 = 104
```

String Operators

The string operator uses the sign "+" to concatenate two or more strings.

```
var FirstName = "Fname"';
```

```
var LastName = "Lname";
var FullName = FirstName + "" + LastName;
```

Operator	Meaning
!=	Not Equal to
==	Equal to
===	Equal to and equal type
<	Less than
>	Greater than
<=	Less than equal to
>=	Greater than equal to

Comparison Operator in JavaScript

Logical Operators in JavaScript

Operator	Property
!	Logical not
||	Logical or
&&	Logical and

Basic JavaScript on the Browser side

When you hear about JavaScript on the browser side, it refers to the client-side, which means the code is run on the machine of the client – the browser. The browser-side components comprise of JavaScript, JavaScript libraries, CSS, images, HMTL, and whatever files downloaded to the browser.

Browser-Side JavaScript Features

JavaScript is important for the web as it is likely to use it to write programs that execute arbitrary computations. You have the opportunity of writing simple scripts such as the search for prime numbers or Fibonacci numbers. However, in the context of web browser and the Web, JavaScript enables programmers to program with the capability of computing sales tax, based on the information provided by the users through an HTML form.

The truth about JavaScript language is in the document-based objects and browser that the language is compatible with. This may sound complex, however, I will explain the significant capabilities of JavaScript on the browser side along with the objects it supports.

- **Controls the Browser** – There are various JavaScript objects that permit the control of the browser behavior. Furthermore, the Window object support means of popping up dialog boxes that display messages for the users. Additionally, users can also input messages. Besides this, JavaScript doesn't provide a method that gives users the opportunity to directly create and manipulate frames inside the browser window. Notwithstanding, you can take advantage of the ability to make HTML animatedly by creating the particular frame layout you want.

- **Interact with HTML Forms** – another significant part of the JavaScript on the browser side is its capability to work together with HTML forms. The ability comes because of the form element and its objects, which contains Text, submit, select, reset, radio, hidden, password, and text area objects. With these elements, you can write and read the values of the elements in the form.

- **Interact with Users** – JavaScript has another feature, which is its ability to define event handlers. Most times, users initiate these events. For instance, when someone moves the mouse through a hyperlink, clicks the submit button, or enters a value. The capability to handle such events is important because programming with graphic interfaces requires an event-driven model.

In addition to these aforementioned features, JavaScript on the browser side has other capabilities such as:

- Changing the displayed image by using the <img> tag to generate an animation effect and image rollover
- It has a window.setTimeout () method, which allows some block of random source code to be performed in the future within a split of a second
- It streamlines the procedure of working and computing with times and dates

JavaScript Framework

Take a moment and consider creating a web application and websites like constructing a house. In building a house, you can decide to create every material you need to start the house from scratch before building without any plans. This will be time-consuming and won't make much sense. One thing you may likely do is to buy pre-manufactured materials such as bricks, woods, countertops, etc. before assembling them based on the blueprint you have.

Coding is like taking it upon yourself to build a house. When you begin coding a website, you can code all areas of the site from scratch without. However, there are certain website features, which gives your website more sense by applying a template. Assuming you want to buy a wheel, it will make to look for one that you can reinvent. This is where JavaScript Frameworks come to the scene.

JavaScript Framework is a collection of JavaScript code libraries, which gives website developers pre-written JavaScript codes to use for their routine programming tasks and features.

You can also refer to it as an application framework, which is written in JavaScript where the developers can manipulate the functions of these codes and reuse them for their own convenience. They are more adaptable for website designing, which is why many developers use them in building websites.

Top JavaScript Framework

Vue.js

This is one of the JavaScript frameworks, which was created to make the user interface development more organized. Created by Evan You, it is the perfect JavaScript framework for beginners because it's quite easy to understand. Furthermore, it focuses on view layers. With Vue.js, you don't need Babel. A Babel is a transpiler with the responsibility of converting JavaScript codes to the old version of ES5 that can run in all browsers. All templates in the Vue.js framework are valid HTML, which makes their integration easier. If you want to develop lightweight apps as a beginner, it is best to start with Vue.js.

Next.js

Another important JavaScript Framework is the Next.js framework, which is an additional tool for server-side rendering. The framework allows developers to simplify the developing process similar to the Vue.js framework.

The features of this JavaScript Framework include page-based client-side routing and automatic splitting of codes. The framework also comes with a full CSS support, which makes styling of the user's interface easier for beginners and professionals.

Ember.js

This framework, which was created a few years ago, is among the most sought JavaScript framework in the web industry. Famous companies such as LinkedIn, Heroku, and Kickstarter use the Ember.js framework in the design of their websites. It also comes with regular updates and offers a complete feature for users. Unlike the Vue.js framework, it is effective for developers who want to develop complex web applications. The focus of this framework is on scalability, which allows developers to use it for both web and mobile projects.

Angular

Google released this JavaScript Framework in 2010 with regular updates and improvements taking place. It is one of the most sought after the framework for many developers because it simplifies the development of websites and apps. For other developers, it is because of its ability to create dynamic web apps.

Chapter Eight: Introduction to PHP

PHP is an acronym for Hypertext Preprocessor. The language is a server-side HTML embedded scripting language. For beginners, it is hard to understand the aforementioned statement, however, let me break it down. When I say the langue is a server-side, I mean the execution of the scripts takes place on the server where the website is hosted. By HTML embedded, it means PHP codes can be used inside HTML code. Alternatively, a scripting language is a programming language, which is interpreted instead of being compiled like C++ and C programming language. Examples of scripting languages include Java, Python, Perl, and Ruby.

You can use PHP language on several platforms including UNIX, Linux, and windows and it supports many databases including Oracle, Sybase, MySQL, etc. furthermore, PHP files contain scripts, HTML tags, and plain text with extensions such as PHP3, PHP, or PHTML. Finally, the software is an open-source program, which is free.

Pre-requisite for learning PHP

If you want to know if there is anything special necessary to know before learning PHP, then the answer to this question is no. Going through the documentation section gives you the necessary information you need. One major reason many find it easy to learn PHP is due to its documentation that every concept is explained in its simplicity.

Additionally, PHP is a simple and straightforward language for anyone to learn. However, if you want to learn web language effectively, it is important to learn the basics of the following languages:

- HTML – This is what PHP sends to the web browser
- MySQL – You need a database to store data
- CSS – You need this to add style to your HTML pages
- JavaScript – To make your pages interactive with the users

If you can equip yourself with these languages, then you can learn PHP effectively.

Getting Started

Before starting this lesson, you should have the following:

- PHP and MySQL installed
- Web Server (Apache)

With these two programs, you can successfully write and execute PHP codes. You can purchase an inexpensive hosting plan that supports MySQL and PHP. However, if you want to save some cash, you can decide to install it on your system. To do this, you have to install WAMP server on your machine for Windows users. After the installation, you can access it through http://localhost in your browser. Ensure you have this set up before starting this course.

PHP Syntax

When I started, I indicated that PHP codes are executed on the server-side. However, every PHP statement begins with <?PHP while ending with ?>. Let us begin with a simple program. You can copy and paste the program below using any text editor before saving it with the file name – index1.php

I named the file to "index1.php" because some root folder already has an index filename as shown in the image below.

Name	Date modified	Type	Size
elijahdokubo	12/10/2018 5:17 PM	File folder	
greaterlight	11/29/2018 10:08 ...	File folder	
mysite	11/7/2018 2:21 AM	File folder	
SpredMax	4/11/2019 11:41 AM	File folder	
wamplangues	3/11/2018 6:21 PM	File folder	
wampthemes	3/11/2018 6:21 PM	File folder	
wordpress	2/14/2019 8:33 AM	File folder	
wordpress-5.0	2/14/2019 8:22 AM	File folder	
add_vhost	11/5/2016 3:44 PM	PHP File	20 KB
favicon	2/4/2019 6:48 AM	Icon	198 KB
index	8/31/2017 6:26 PM	PHP File	31 KB
test_sockets	9/21/2015 6:30 PM	PHP File	1 KB
testmysql	12/13/2016 2:50 PM	PHP File	1 KB
wordpress-5.0	12/10/2018 4:54 PM	Compressed (zipp...	11,108 KB

```
<html>
<head>
</head>
<body>

<?php
    /* This line contains a comment
    Which span to
    several lines */

    //This comment is a line comment
```

```
    //echo prints the statement onto the screen
    echo "Hello World, Welcome to PHP Programming!"
?>


</body>
</html>
```

When executed, you should have the output as:

Hello World, Welcome to PHP Programming!

Variables in PHP Programming

I will go directly into the PHP variable declaration statement as we have dealt with variables in different chapters in this book. Every variable in PHP normally begins with the dollar ($) sign. Most beginners make the mistake of not including the dollar ($) at the beginner. I know you won't make that mistake.

```
<?PHP
    $variable1 = 280;
    $variable2 = "PHP Programming";
?>
```

We first declare variable1 with the value 280. However, the second is a string variable with value as "PHP Programming"

It is important to note that every statement n PHP ends with a semicolon. You will get an error whenever you don't include a semicolon to indicate the ending of a statement.

Variable Rules in PHP

- A variable name always begins with an underscore (_) or a letter
- A variable name must not include a space (s)

- Variable names can only have an underscore or alpha-numerical character

String Variables

String variables are important especially if you want to manipulate and store text in your program. The code below assigns the text "Welcome to PHP Programming" to the variable beginner and prints out the content to the screen.

```php
<?php
    $beginner = 'Welcome to PHP Programming';
    echo $beginner;
?>
```

Output

← → C ⌂ ⓘ localhost/index1

Welcome to PHP Programming

Strlen () function

Perhaps you want to determine the string length of a word or sentence, the strlen function is what you need. Consider the example below.

```php
<?php
    echo strlen("Today is the best day of your life. Programming is a lifelong skill and PHP is all your need");
?>
```

The outcome will be the string length of the text including the signs, space, characters). In this situation, the result will be 92 as shown below.

← → C ⌂ ⓘ localhost/index1

92

Operators in PHP Programming

In this segment, I will rundown through the basic operators in PHP. I will look at the assignment, arithmetic, comparison, logical, and concatenation operators.

Assignment operators

Operator	Examples	Large notation
%=	p%=q	p=p%q
*=	p*=q	p=p*q
.=	p.=q	p=p.q
/=	p/=q	p=p/q
+=	p+=q	p=p+q
=	p=p	p=q
-=	p-=q	p=p-q

Logical Operators

Operator	Description	Example
!	not	p=9 q=9 !(p==q) returns false
&&	and	p=9 q=9 (p < 10 && q> 1) returns true

197

||	or	p=9
		q=9
		(p==5 || q==5) returns true

Arithmetic Operators

Operator	Description	Example	Result
+	Addition	a=8 a+5	13
−	Subtraction	a=17 20-a	3
/	Division	a = 40 40/2	20
*	Multiplication	a=7 a*5	35
++	Increment	a=9 a++	a=10
--	Decrement	a=14 a--	a=13
%	Modulus (division remainder)	56%6	2

Comparison Operator

Operator	Description	Example
==	is equal to	48==49 returns false

!=	is not equal	48!=49 returns true
<	is less than	48<49 returns true
<=	is less than or equal to	48<=49 returns true
<>	is not equal	48<>49 returns true
>	is greater than	48>49 returns false
>=	is greater than or equal to	48>=49 returns false

Conditional Statements in PHP Programming

At times, you may want to make decisions that require different actions when writing a program, conditional statement plays a huge role to perform some decision. In PHP language, we have the if statement, if... else statement, the if...elseif... else statement. In this section, I will expand on these statements including their syntax.

If Statement

The statement is required to execute a line of code as far as the condition stated is true. Consider the example below.

```
<?php
```

```
$number= 23;
if($number='23')
echo "Wake up! Time to begin Your Programming lesson.";
?>
```

In the statement above, we first declare allocate the value 23 to the variable "number". The if statement now evaluates if the variable "number" is equal to 23 since it is true, it will return:

Wake up! Time to begin Your Programming lesson.

The If...else statement

This condition examines two different statements and evaluates one depending on the condition specified. A simple English illustration will be: buy a donut if there is no pizza available.

```
<?php
```

```
    $decision1='Donut';
    if($decision1 == 'Donut') {
        echo 'Buy Donut when coming';
    } else {
        echo 'Buy Pizza when coming';
    }
?>
```

The output will be:

Buy Donut when coming

Let's twist the same code and consider the output.

```
<?php
    $decision1='Donut';
```

```
    if($decision1 == 'Don') {
        echo 'Buy Donut when coming';
    } else {
        echo 'Buy Pizza when coming';
    }
?>
```

The output will be:

Buy Pizza when coming

It doesn't work on string alone but you can also use it on number operations.

The if ... else if...else statement

You can use this statement to select a single option from a different line of codes. The example below will explain better.

```
<?php
    $number1=10;
```

```
    $number2=10;
    if($number1 == 8) {
        echo 'The expression is true';
    } elseif($number2 == $number2) {
        echo 'The second expression is true';
    } else {
        echo 'The two if statements are true';
    }
?>
```

The output:

The second if statement is true

Switch Statement

The statement allows you to change the course of the program flow. It is best suited when you want to perform various actions on different conditions. Consider the example below.

```php
<html>
<body>
<?php
    $a=2;
    switch ($a)
    {
        case 1:
            echo 'The number is 10';
        break;
        case 2:
            echo 'The number is 20';
        break;
        case 3:
            echo 'The number is 30';
        break;
        default:
            echo 'There is no number that match';
    }
?>
</body>
</html>
```

Output:

The number is 30

Explanation

In the example above, we declare the variable "a" to be 3. The switch statement has some block of codes, with case or default. If the value of the case is equivalent to the variable $a, it will execute the statement within that line and then break. However, if the value of the case is not equivalent to any of the variable, it will break from the case before executing the default code block.

Conclusion

PHP language isn't restricted to professional web browsers alone. You don't have to be an IT administrative professional to learn it. Similar to any scripting language, it may seem complicated at the first time; however, if you preserver, you will discover it is an interesting language to learn. Learning PHP programming is the perfect way of understanding the server-side world.

Writing PHP code is not something intimidating if you start from the foundation as I have done in this book. PHP language is one of the languages you don't need anyone to teach you as long as you are ready to learn everything. In this book, you have learned everything you need to get your environment ready, variables, conditional statements, and much more.

Chapter Nine: Python Programming Language

Introduction

Python Language is one of the easiest and straightforward object-oriented languages to learn. Its syntax is simple, thereby making it simple for beginners to learn and understand the language with ease. In this chapter, I will cover several aspects of the Python programing language. This programming guide is for beginners who want to learn a new language. However, if you are an advanced programmer, you will also learn something.

Guido Van Rossum developed the Python language but the implementation began in 1989. Initially, you could have thought, it was named after the Python snake; however, it was named after a comedy television show called "Monty Python's Flying Circus."

Features of Python

There are certain features that make the python programming language unique among other programming languages. The summary is displayed in the diagram below.

1. **Easy to learn** – Because python is a high-level and expressive language, it is easy for everyone – including you to learn and understand irrespective of their programming level – beginners to advanced programming

2. **Readable** – It is quite easy to read the language

3. **Open source** – The language is an open-source language

4. **Cross-platform** – This means it is available and you runnable on different operating systems including UNIX, Linux, Windows, Mac, etc. This has contributed to its portability.

5. **Free** – The language is downloadable without paying anything. Furthermore, not only can you download it, you can it for various applications. The software is distributable freely.

6. **Large standard library** – Python has its standard library, which contains various functions and code, which you can add to your code.

7. **Supports exception handling** – Most programming languages have this exception handling feature. However, an exception is a situation that takes place in the course of program execution and has the tendency to disrupt the flow of the program. With python exception handling feature, you can write less error code while testing various situation that may lead to an exception in the future.

8. **Memory management** – The language also supports automatic memory management, which means it clear and free memory automatically. There is no need for clearing the memory on your own when you remember.

Uses of Python

Most beginners before choosing to learn a programming language first consider what the uses of such language are. However, there are various applications of the python language in a real-world situation. These include:

1. **Data Analysis** – You can use python to develop data analysis and visualization in the form of charts
2. **Game development** – Today, the game industry is a huge market that yields billions of dollars per year. It may interest you to know that you can use python to develop interesting games.
3. **Machine learning** – We have various machine learning applications that are written using the python language. For instance, products recommendation in websites such as eBay, Flipkart, Amazon, etc. uses a machine-learning algorithm, which recognizes the user's interest. Another area of machine learning is a voice and facial recognition on your phone.
4. **Web development** – You didn't see this coming. Well, web frameworks such as Flask and Django are based on the python language. With Python, you can write backend programming logics, manage database, map URLs, etc.
5. **Embedded applications** – You can use python to develop embedded applications

How to Install Python Programming Language

It is very easy to install python on your system. Since it is cross-platform, you don't need to crack your brain. By cross-platform, I mean you can install it on Ubuntu, Mac, UNIX, Windows, etc. To install it on your system, you can visit this link https://www.python.org/downloads. You can download it here and it comes with the option of choosing your particular operating system. So the installation process is not complicated. After downloading the software according to your operating system, follow the onscreen instruction to complete the process.

Since you are a beginner, I will teach you how to install the PyCharm, which is a common IDE used for python programming. IDE stands for an integrated development environment. The IDE contains a debugger, interpreter or compiler, and a code editor.

Installation of PyCharm IDE

First, go to this address – https://www.jetbrains.com/pycharm/download/ to download the edition you want. After this, install the downloaded file. If you are using a MAC system, you have to double click the .dmg file before dragging PyCharm to the application folder. However, for windows users, you have to open the .exe file before following the direction on the screen.

Launching PyCharm

For windows users, after installing the .exe file, you will see the PyCharm icon on the desktop depending on the option you selected during installation. You can also go to your program files

> Jetbrains >PyCharm2017 and look for the PyCharm.exe file to launch PyCharm.

Python Program Beginning

Once you open the IDE and give a name to your project, you can start programming. You can begin with this simple program

```
# This Python program prints Welcome to Python Programming
on the screen
print('Welcome to Python Programming')
```

If you did that, you should have the following

```
Welcome to Python Programming
```

Comments in Python

If you observe from the first line, I began with "#" whenever you see that it is a comment and in Python, it doesn't change the program outcome. Comments are very important because it helps you to easily read the program by providing further explanation of the codes in English for everyone to understand.

Comments can be written in two ways in Python. This could be single or multiple line comments. The single-line comment uses the #, which is an example of the previous code. However, the multiple line comment uses three single quotes (''') at the beginning and end respectively.

```
'''
Example of multiple line comment
'''
```

Let me use a real example to explain both the single and multiple line comment.

```
'''
Sample program to illustrate multiple line comment
Pay close attention
'''
print("We are making progress")

# Second print statement
print("Do you agree?")

print("Python Programming for Beginners") # Third print
statement
```

Output:

```
We are making progress
Do you agree?
```

Python Variables

We use variables to store data in programming. Variable creation is very simple to implement in Python. In python, you have to declare the variable name and value together. For instance

Number1 = 140 #number1 is of integer type

str = "Beginner" #str is of string type

Variable Name Convention in Python

Another name for a variable name is an identifier. Python has some laid down rules when it has to do with naming variables. These rules differ from other programming languages.

1. Variable names must always start with an underscore (-) or a letter. For example, _number1, number1,
2. Variable names cannot contain special characters such as #, %, $, etc. however, they can have underscore and alphanumeric characters
3. A variable name cannot begin with a number. For instance, 3number is invalid
4. It is case sensitive. For instance, number1 and NUMBER2 are entirely different variable names in python

Python Variable examples

```
Number1 = 589
Str = "Python Programming"
Print (Number1)
Print (Str)
```

The output will be:

```
589
Python Programming
```

Multiple Assignment

You can also allocate several variables to a single expression in python. Consider the example below:

```
Profit = returns = yields = 35
print (Profit)
print (yield)
print (returns)
```

Output

```
35
35
35
```

Let us consider another example

```
A, B, C = 35, 8, 90
print (A)
print (B)
print (C)
```

Output

```
35
8
90
```

Concatenation and plus Operation on variables

```
A = 44
B = 68
print (A + B)

c = "Welcome"
d = "Home"
print (c + " " + d)
```

Output

```
112
Welcome Home
```

However, if you decide to use the + operator in conjunction with a and c, it will display an error such as unsupported operand type (s) for +: 'int'

Data Types in Python

The purpose is to define the type of data a variable accommodate. For instance, "welcome home" is a string data type while 234 is an integer data type. In Python, data types are divided into two different groups. We have the immutable data types, whose values are unchangeable. They include tuple, string, and numbers. The other group is the mutable data types, whose values are changeable and they include sets, dictionaries, and list. In this book, my focus will be on the immutable data types.

Numbers

When working with numbers, python supports floats, integers, and complex numbers. Float numbers are those with decimal points such as 9.9, 4.2, 42.9, etc. An integer is the opposite of float because it does not have a decimal point attached to it. For instance, 3, 35, 89, etc. however, a compound number contain an imaginary and real part such as 7+10j, etc.

Let's demonstrate the use of numbers in a python program

```
# Python program to show how we can use numbers

# declaring the variables number1 and number2 as integer
```

```
number1 = 78
number2 = 12
print(number1+number2)

# declaring a and b as float data type
a = 15.9
b = 5.8
print(a-b)

# declaring x and y as complex numbers
x = 5 + 2j
y = 9 + 6j
print(y-x)
```

Output

```
100
10.1
4 + 4j
```

Strings

This is a series of characters enclosed within a special character. In Python, you have the option of using a single or double quote to represent a string. There are various means of creating strings in python.

- You have the option of a single quote '

- You can use a double quote ”
- You can use a triple-double quotes “”””

```
# Ways of creating strings in Python
str = 'single string example'
print(str)


str2 = "double string example"
print(str2)


# multi-line string
str3 = """ Triple double-quote string"""
print(str3)


str4 = '''This is Python Programming '''
print(str4)
```

```
Single string example
double string example
Triple double-quote string
  Beginnersbook.com
This is Python Programming
```

Tuple

Tuple works like a list but the difference is that in a tuple, the objects are unchangeable. The elements of a tuple are unchangeable once assigned. However, in the case of a list, the element is changeable.

In order to create tuple in python, you have to place all the elements in a parenthesis () with a comma separating it. Let me use an example to illustrate tuple in python.

```
# tuple of strings
bioDate = ("John", "M", "Lawson")
print(bioData)


# tuple of int, float, string
Data_New = (1, 2.8, "John Lawson")
print(Date_New)


# tuple of string and list
details = ("The Programmer", [1, 2, 3])
print(details)


# tuples inside another tuple
# nested tuple
Details2 = ((2, 3, 4), (1, 2, "John"))
```

```
Print(details2)
```

Output will be:

```
("John", "M", "Lawson")
(1, 2.8, "John Lawson")
("The Programmer", 1, 2, 3)
((2, 3, 4), (1, 2, "John"))
```

Control Statement in Python Programming

There are various control statements used in Python to make a decision.

If Statement

The statement prints out a message if a specific condition is satisfied. The format or syntax is as follow:

If condition:

    Line of codes

```
flag = True
if flag==True:
   print("Welcome")
   print("To")
   print("Python Programming")
```

Output

```
Welcome
To
Python Programming
```

Consider another example

```
number1 = 180
if number1 < 290:
    print("number1 is less than 290")
```

Output

number1 is less than 290

If-else statement

in our previous example, we only test a particular condition, what if you want to test two different conditions. That is where the "if-else statement" comes to play. In Python, the statement executes a particular statement if it is true but if it's not true, it executes the other statement.

Syntax

If conditions

Statement1

Else

   Statement2

Let us use our last example to illustrate this.

```
number1 = 180
if number1 > 290:
    print("number1 is greater than 290")
else
    print ("number1 is less than 290")
```

Output

number1 is less than 290

```
Number1 = 15
if number1 % 4 == 0:
    print("the Number is an Even Number")
else:
    print("The Number is an Odd Number")
```

Output:

The Number is an Odd Number

Bonus Programs

```
# Program to display the Fibonacci sequence depending on the
number the user wants

# For a different result, change the values
numb1 = 12

# uncomment to take input from the user
#num1 = int(input("How many times? "))

# first two terms
a1 = 0
a2 = 1
count = 0

# Verify if the number of times is valid
if numb1 <= 0:
   print("Please enter a positive integer")
elif numb1 == 1:
   print("Fibonacci sequence up to",numb1,":")
   print(a1)
else:
   print("Fibonacci sequence up to",numb1,":")
   while count < numb1:
     print(a1,end=' , ')
```

```
        nth = a1 + a2
        # update values
        a1 = a2
        a2 = nth
        count += 1
```

What do you think the output will be?

Fibonacci sequence up to 12 :

0, 1, 1, 2, 3, 5, 8, 13, 21, 34, 55, 89

Conclusion on Python Programming

So far, you have learned the fundamentals of Python Programming. However, there are advanced topics such as functions, recursions, python OOP, python constructors, etc. My goal is that you have the basic knowledge of the language to equip you in other programming languages. Now you know how to write a program in Python and use the language conveniently. I am convinced that you can install Python on a different system. I have also covered how to use the control flow tools such as if statement and if...else statement.

Python is not a hard language and at that, you should invest your time to dive into advanced programming.

Glossary

Algorithm – A series of instruction aimed at solving a single problem.

Boolean – An expression whose statements can only be true or false. It is sometimes used in combination with AND, OR, NOT, XOR, and NOR operators. They are also called comparison expression or relational expression.

Class – A set of related objects sharing the same features in the course of a program

Code – A program code or source code written as a set of instructions under a particular language

Compilation – A process of creating a program using code, which is written in a particular computer language. When a program undergoes the compilation process, the computer understands the codes and run the program without any programming software. C++ is an example of a compiler

Compile – The process of creating executable from code written in a particular language

Compile-time – The total time taken for the compiler to compile a particular program

Compiler - A software that converts codes written into programs

Constants – A constant is a term in the course of a program whose value does not change throughout the program execution. It is different from a variable whose value changes. Constants remain fixed and can be a character, number, and string.

Data types – This is a classification of a data type in a program. Data types include integers, String, Boolean, etc. Unlike humans, computers cannot differentiate between a number and a letter unless   specified.

Array – This is a group or list of similar data values, which are categorized. Although the values are of the same data type, however, their position is not the same. For instance, the student of a particular class can be an array but their results after the exam will be different.

Declaration – A statement that describes a function, variable or any identifier in the course of a program

Developer – An individual whose job is to create or work on the development of a product or services. Developers use various programming languages to develop these products

Exception – An anomalous and unexpected condition encountered while executing a program. Another word for an exception is an error and it causes the code to execute.

Expression – A group of symbols, letters, and number that represent a variable. An expression is used in various programming languages with each having its own rules.

False – A Boolean value in programming that is used when the outcome of the local statement is not true

Function – A group of instructions used in programming languages to return a single or set of results.

Immutable Object – An object which is unchangeable after created. These are common in object-oriented programming languages like Java

Increment – In programming, the process of increasing the numerical value of a particular variable. It is the opposite of decrement.

Inheritance - This concept involves an object receiving the same features or properties of another object that supports it.

Interpreter – In programming, a programming language doesn't require undergoing the compilation process before its execution

JavaScript - A scripting language that allows developers to insert code into a website page. They are used to perform various advanced tasks such as creating a calendar, printing the time and date

Keywords – These are reserved words used by a programming language and have special meaning. Each programming language has its own reserved keywords, which must not be used as a variable name. For instance, "continue", "static," "if," "return," and "default" are some of the keywords reserved in C programming language

Loop – A series of instruction that repeats itself pending when a specific condition is met before stopping the process. Loop is one of the basic concepts in programming. Almost all programming language use loop to execute complete decisions.

Object-Oriented Programming (OOP) – A model with data structure with data in the form of fields and functions that can be applied to it

Objects – A combination of related constants, variables, and other data structures, which can be manipulated together. Example, the gender of students in a particular school

Operand – A term used to represent an object in which various manipulations can take place. For instance, in the expression "num1+num2+num3", num1, num2, and num3 are operands.

Operators – A term used to describe operations that can take place in n operand or object. For instance, "a*b+C" in the expression, * and + are operators, which perform a certain operation on the operands.

Polymorphism - The ability of a particular programming language to interpret objects in various ways depending on their data type or class.

Program – a collection of instruction that must be executed serially. The CPU process the program before its execution. A program, also called software sometimes contains a couple of lines to millions of lines with each providing different instructions. The instructions are called source code whereas the act of computer programming is program coding.

Programming language - This is an artificial language aimed at controlling the operation and functionality of a computer similar to the English language, they have rules (syntactic and semantic rules).

Reserved Words – These are unique words reserved for a particular programming language. Same as keywords

Statement – It represents a single line of code, which is written to express an action that must be carried out in that programming language. For instance, $Q = R+8$

Syntax – These are rules that a particular programming language has. Different programming languages may have the same functions, features, and capabilities; however, they may have different syntax. For instance, the syntax for display a text to the screen in C++ is different from that of a Java program

Variable – A storage location used to save temporary data during a program. Unlike constants, you can manipulate, store, and display a variable value. For instance, an integer variable "number1" stores a value like 45. However, if after this, you use the same name and store 67 as the value, it takes the new value and discards the old value (45)

Exercises for all Languages

SQL Test Questions

Q 1 - Which of the SQL statements below is not true?

    A. SQL statements can be written on more than a single line.
    B. SQL statements are not case sensitive
    C. Clauses must be on a separate line
    D. Keywords cannot be split across lines

Q 2 – Consider the code below

STUDENTS (StudID, FirstName, LastName, Email,

PhoneNum, DoB, Subject, Total_Score);

Which statement below will display the student full name with a column heading "Name"

    A. SELECT FirstName || LastName as "Name" from
        STUDENTS;
    B. SELECT FirstName, LastName FROM STUDENTS;
    C. SELECT Name FROM STUDENTS;
    D. SELECT FirstName, LastName FROM STUDENTS;

Q3 – Consider the code below

STUDENTS (StudID, FirstName, LastName, Email,

PhoneNum, DoB, Subject, Total_Score);

Which of the query will display subjects from the table?

- A. SELECT ALL subjects FROM STUDENTS;
- B. SELECT Subjects FROM STUDENTS;
- C. SELECT * Subject FROM STUDENTS;
- D. SELECT Subject OR Total_Score FROM STUDENTS;

Q4 – Consider the code below

Students (StudID, FirstName, LastName, Email,

PhoneNum, DoB, Subject, Total_Score);

Which of the query will display students offering only "MTH112) subjects from the table?

- A. SELECT StudID, FirstName, LastName FROM Students
  WHERE Subject = "MTH112";
- B. SELECT StudID, FirstName, LastName FROM Students
  WHERE subject is "MTH112";
- C. SELECT StudID, FirstName, LastName WHERE subject
  = "MTH112";
- D. SELECT StudID, FirstName, LastName FROM Students;

Q5 – Consider the Schema below

Students (StudID, FirstName, LastName, Email,

PhoneNum, DoB, Subject, Total_Score);

A. SELECT FirstName FROM Students WHERE FirstName like "A";

B. SELECT FirstName FROM Students WHERE FirstName like "%A%";

C. SELECT FirstName FROM Students WHERE FirstName like "%A";

D. SELECT FirstName FROM Students WHERE FirstName like "A%";

C++ Test Question

Q1 – A trigraph character starts with

A. #

B. ?

C. ??

D. ##

Q 2 - The default access specifier for class members is

A. Private

B. Protected

C. Public

D. None

Q3 – C++ doesn't support the following inheritance

A. Multilevel

B. Hierarchical

C. Hybrid

D. There is no answer

Q4 – From the following statement, which of them is true concerning inline function?

A. It doesn't execute faster when compared to normal function

B. It executes faster due to its higher priority when compared to normal function

C. It performs faster because it is treated as a macro internally

D. None of the above

Q5 – Which of the statement below is the true definition of an abstract class?

A. It is a class, which must have a pure virtual function defined outside the class

B. It is a class, which may not have a pure virtual function

C. It is a class, which must have at least a pure virtual function

D. It is a class, which must have all pure virtual functions

Q 6 - Which of the following is not a reserved word in C++?

A. extends

B. friend

C. this

D. volatile

Q7 – determine the output of the program

```cpp
#include<iostream>

using namespace std;
class ab {

  public:
    int p;

    ab(int p) {
      p = p;
    }
};

main() {
  ab c(5);

  cout<<c.a;
}
```

A. Garbage

B. 5

C. Compile error "a" declared twice

D. Error at the statement a = a;

C Programming Test Questions

Q1 – Consider the simple program below?

```
#include<stdio.h>

main()
{
  int const a = 8;
    p++;
  printf("%d",p);
}
```

    A. 6

    B. 9

    C. Runtime error

    D. Compile error

Q2 – determine the program

```
#include<stdio.h>

main()
{
  char p[]="welcome", q[]="welcome";

  if(p==q){
        printf("equal strings");
        }
```

```
}
```

A. No output

B. Unequal strings

C. Equal string

D. Compilation error

Q3 - Consider the code snippet below, choose the right output.

```
#include<stdio.h>
main()
{
  int p = 5, q = 3, r = 4;
    printf("p = %d, q = %d\n", p, q, r);
}
```

A. compile error

B. p=5, q=3

C. p=5, q=3, 0

D. p=5, q=3, c = 0

Q4 - determine the output of the program

```
#include<stdio.h>
main()
{
int p = 1;
double q;
float r = 1.3;
```

```
    q = p + r;
    printf("%.2lf", q);
}
```

    A. 2.3

    B. 2.0

    C. 2.30

    D. Error

Q5 – determine the output

```
#include<stdio.h>
main()
{
    enum { Germany, is=9, Excellent };
    printf("%d %d", Germany, Excellent);
}
```

    A. Compile error

    B. 0 1

    C. 0 2

    D. 0 8

Q6 – determine the output of the program

```
#include<stdio.h>
main()
{
    char p = 'B'+265;
    printf("%c", p);
```

```
}
```

A. Compile error

B. Overflow error during runtime

C. B

D. A

Q7 – determine the output of the program

```
#include<stdio.h>

main()
{
   short unsigned int a = 0;
   printf("%u\n", a--);
}
```

A. 65568

B. 32789

C. Compile error

D. 0

Q8 – determine the output of the program

```
#include<stdio.h>
main()
{
   unsigned q = 5, n=&q, *p = n+0;
   printf("%u",*p);
}
```

A. Address of p

B. Address of n

C. Address of q

D. 5

Q9 – Consider the code below, determine the output of the program

```c
#include<stdio.h>
main()
{
  int p = 8;
    if(q==8)
    {
      if(p==8) break;
      printf("You are Right");
    }
    printf("Hello");
}
```

   A. You are Right

   B. You are RightHello

   C. Hello

   D. Compile error

Q10 – Consider the code, determine the program output

```c
#include<stdio.h>

main()
{
```

```
int a = 8;
if(a=8)
{
  if(a=8) printf("You Are Right");
}
printf("Hello");
}
```

A. Compile error

B. You Are RightHello

C. Hello

D. You Are Right

Q11 – Consider the code snippet, determine the output of the program

```
#include<stdio.h>
main()
{
  for(4;5;6)
    printf("Welcome");
}
```

A. Compile error

B. No output

C. Prints "Welcome" once

D. Infinite loop

Q12 – Consider the code below, what will be the value of a?

```
int a = ~1;
```

    A. 2

    B. -1

    C. 1

    D. -2

JavaScript Programming Test Question

Q 1 –from the statement below, which is true concerning the features of JavaScript?

    A. JavaScript is integrated with Java

    B. JavaScript is a lightweight, interpreted programming language

    C. All of the above

Q 2 –identify the correct feature of JaveScript in the statement below?

    A. JavaScript is corresponding to and embedded with HTML

    B. Open and cross-platform

    C. A and B are True

    D. All of the above

Q 3 - Which of the statement below is true of the advantage of JavaScript?

   A. Less server interaction

   B. Increased interactivity

   C. Immediate feedback to the visitors

   D. All of the above

Q 4 - Which of the statement below is true about variable naming conventions in JavaScript?

B - Variable names are case sensitive.

A - JavaScript variable names must begin with underscore or letter.

C – A and B is True

D - None of the above

Q 5 – Is it possible to access Cookie using JavaScript?

   A. True

   B. False

Q 6 - Which statement below is true regarding cookie handling in JavaScript?

   A. JavaScript can modify, create, read, and delete the cookie (s) of a webpage

   B. JavaScript can control cookies via the property of the cookie.

   C. A and B is True

   D. None of the above

Q 7 – Identify the correct syntax to redirect a url using JavaScript?

   A. browser.location='http://www.newlocation.com';

   B. document.location='http://www.newlocation.com';

   C. navigator.location='http://www.newlocation.com';

   D. window.location='http://www.newlocation.com';

Q 8 – Choose the right syntax to print a page using JavaScript

   A. browser.print();

   B. document.print();

   C. navigator.print();

   D. window.print();

Q 9 – Identify the valid type of function supported by JavaScript?

   A. anonymous function
   B. Both of the above
   C. named function
   D. None of the above

Summary of the Book

In Java Programming, you will acquire every information you need concerning data types, object-oriented programming, and control structures in Java. You will learn more than the codes. However, the next chapter challenges you on learning JavaScript, one of the most common scripting languages in the world. Furthermore, PHP will help you master the art of writing quality code. You will discover the basic syntax when writing PHP programs. In the SQL chapter, you will learn the nitty-gritty of creating a database and table easily. Furthermore, you will learn how to insert, select, and perform various actions on a table. This book indeed is a must-have for any serious programmer. Polish your programming skill by buying this book. Invest in your future.

The book covers programming topics such as:

- Prerequisites for learning each language
- Features of the language
- The concepts of different programming language
- Variables of the different programming language
- Where the language is applicable in our today world

The book is well arranged for easy understanding. Indeed the book is a comprehensive guide to understanding eight programming languages to start coding your way to the top.

Don't forget to brush your knowledge by going through the exercise page. It contains serious of questions to test your knowledge of each programming topic you have covered. Before you know it, you have mastered and the results on the screen will tell your success story. So what are you waiting for? Let the programming begin!

www.ingramcontent.com/pod-product-compliance
Lightning Source LLC
LaVergne TN
LVHW051226050326
832903LV00028B/2259